Praise for *Love*

'Deni's effervescence that we've seen and loved on social media shines through in *Love This for You*. They share their experiences with generosity, affection, thoughtfulness, and a genuine desire to help others to heal and grow. While some difficult topics are tackled, it is balanced by a delicious playfulness. Deni has an important story to tell, which lends itself to an increasing need for diverse voices in Australian literature, and they've done so in a way that is sometimes missing in memoirs – fun!' – Yumiko Kadota

'One of the warmest, most captivating voices of our generation. Deni is a force for empathy, light, love and progress.' – Michelle Andrews

'As a queer child of immigrants who dreamed of being all that I could be myself, this book spoke to my soul. I felt my heart drop, and I felt it soar. I smiled and I cried. A privilege, an eye-opener and a heart-warmer, this book covers the conversations we need to have, but don't, in a way rich in humour, education and importantly love. And I love this for anyone who gets to read this.' – Maria Thattil

'Deni's story is a masterclass in authenticity, spirit and courage.' – Mia Freedman

'I have watched an amazing transformation – Deni literally bloomed before our eyes from the start of that long, hard lockdown in 2020. Delightful and inspiring. If you have wondered, like me, how they did it, how they got there and are now beaming with light, here are the pages that explain, entertain and have laughs and lessons for us all. A raw and engaging read that makes me want to sparkle even brighter.' – Dannii Minogue

'A life-affirming love letter. By guiding you through their sensory journey of self-discovery, Deni supports and challenges you to start your own.' – Narelda Jacobs

The author would like to acknowledge and pay respects to the Wadawurrung people, and the Wurundjeri people of the Kulin nation, the Traditional Owners and Custodians of the lands on which this book was written. Sovereignty was never ceded; this land always was, and always will be, Aboriginal land.

About the author

Deni Todorović (they/them) is a Queer content creator, activist, creative director, podcast host, former celebrity stylist and former fashion editor of *Cosmopolitan Australia*. They have worked in fashion for more than a decade, including at mastheads such as *British Vogue*, *InStyle*, *Cosmopolitan UK* and for luxury brands Net-a-Porter and Burberry. As a content creator they have also collaborated with local and international brands ranging from American Express, Fenty Beauty, Levi's and Sephora to Kmart, Camilla, The Body Shop and The Iconic. They are proudly a part of the global movement to de-gender fashion, as was displayed through their work as creative and fashion director for the opening show of 2021's Melbourne Fashion Week.

Deni continues to carve out their own space on social media to inform, inspire and educate their audience around gender identity, pronouns and self-expression via fashion, leading always with the values of empathy, love and kindness. They also host a weekly fashion podcast for the Mamamia network, titled *What Are You Wearing?*

You can find them on Instagram @stylebydeni

Deni Todorović

LOVE THIS FOR YOU

How to Rewrite the Rules and Live Authentically

PANTERA
PRESS

PANTERA
PRESS

First published in 2022 by Pantera Press Pty Limited
www. PanteraPress.com

A Cataloguing-in-Publication entry for this work is available from the National Library of Australia.

ISBN 978-0-6452401-5-3 (Paperback)
ISBN 978-0-6452401-6-0 (eBook)

Cover Design: George Saad
Internal Illustrations: Jes Layton
Acquiring Editor: Tom Langshaw
Copyeditor: Cristina Briones
Proofreader: Camha Pham
Typesetting: Kirby Jones
Author Photo: Monika Berry; hair and makeup by Tess Holmes
Printed and bound in Australia by McPherson's Printing Group

The paper this book is printed on is certified against the Forest Stewardship Council® Standards. McPherson's Printing Group holds FSC® chain of custody certification SA-COC-005379. FSC® promotes environmentally responsible, socially beneficial and economically viable management of the world's forests.

This book is dedicated to those who felt lost,
willing themselves to be found.

You've found me.
Now it's my turn to help you find yourself! x

CONTENTS

Deni's Dictionary aka a glossary of key terms   ix

Introduction: Turning on the light switch   1

1. Where it all began   13
2. It runs in the family   37
3. The uniforms that bound us   61
4. Let's talk about sex   89
    A letter on gender   115
5. Matters of the heart   121
6. The hustle   153
7. Honouring your vessel   183
8. Home truths   215
9. Spirituality, surrender and devotion   241
10. Power in liberation   273

Epilogue   297

Acknowledgements   301

DENI'S DICTIONARY
aka a glossary of key terms

Before we begin, I'd like you to know that I speak, and write, in a distinct way. I'm fluent in multiple languages, and my everyday vocabulary draws from a range of sources, including my cultural background, Queer subcultures and pop culture references. I recognise that not every reader will be familiar with these frames of reference, so to kick us off, here's a non-exhaustive list of some words you'll find in this book, their meaning and context, and why I wanted to include them.

AFAB and AMAB

These are the acronyms for 'assigned female at birth' and 'assigned male at birth', describing the sex category that we were placed into when we were born based on our physical characteristics (even though there is biological diversity in sex beyond this binary of male/female). These terms are used to highlight that our gender – how we choose to identify and how we present – can differ from the sex we were labelled with at birth. If you're feeling a bit lost, don't worry: I'll explain all of this, and more, later!

BIPOC
Black, Indigenous (and) people of colour

Bitch
I know that this word can be a touchy subject for some, so I want to approach it with care. While it can so often be used in a pejorative way, as a misogynistic slur, when I use 'bitch' it's coming from a place of Queer vernacular, from powerful women, transgender and cisgender, and drag queens – and it's a compliment of the highest order. If I call someone 'that bitch', that means they're a bona fide queen. I respect if the use of this word makes you uncomfortable, especially if you're a woman; I want to be clear here that it's coming from a place of love and respect.

D&M
The very nineties acronym given to 'deep and meaningful', describing the types of conversations that often happen at night, between two good friends, going deep on all the subjects closest to their heart. Think too much alcohol, the smokers' section of a nightclub, and nightclub bathrooms of the femme variety.

DMs
Direct messages on social media

Enby
A colloquial expression for a non-binary person, someone whose gender identity exists outside the binary of female/male.

Henny
In laypeople's terms, 'henny' is gay/Queer for 'honey'. *Hey, henny…*

ILYSM
I love you so much

IRL
In real life

Mazel tov
A Jewish expression meaning 'good luck and congratulations'; a celebratory statement that many humans will be familiar with as it's made its way into everyday English. I grew up admiring Jewish women on television, from Barbra Streisand to Bette Midler and Fran Drescher, and many strong Jewish women have been an important part of my life. Jewish people and 'wogs' share many cultural values, in particular a strong connection to family and faith.

MVP
Most valuable player

Okurr
'Okurr' is basically a sassy, trilled way of saying 'okay'. While many credit the embellishment to Cardi B, I first became aware of it via Khloé Kardashian. It wasn't until I started watching *RuPaul's Drag Race* that I realised the term originated in the Queer community, most likely in the Black and Latinx ballroom scene of New York City in the late twentieth century. So much of contemporary Queer vernacular is drawn from AAVE (African-

American Vernacular English) spoken by Black Queer people, Black women (including Black trans women) and Queer people of colour, and there's an ongoing debate in Queer communities about the appropriation of this language.

Queen
A compliment of the highest order in Queer vernacular.

Wog
I was very young when I first heard this word: from parents, relatives and friends who self-identified as wogs, and as a slur from the mouths of non-wogs. It's worth noting that the racialised context of this word differs in the UK, but in this book it's used to describe migrants mostly from Southern Europe since the postwar wave of migration in the fifties and sixties. As with many racial slurs, 'wog' has been reclaimed by community, and it is for this reason that throughout my life, myself and many humans around me have used this word with great pride, affection and endearment. If it makes you uncomfortable, I respect that, particularly if you're an ethnic person reading this; I would also ask that you respect my desire to reclaim the term.

YOLO
You only live once

INTRODUCTION

Turning on the light switch

Let me take you back to March 2020, a month I'm sure many of us would rather forget. (I'm throwing you in the deep end right away. Those who know me will tell you that my favourite conversations are ones that get real deep, real quick, with no lube. Bottoms up!) On yet another mundane lockdown morning, I found myself sitting under the doona in my bedroom, in a pair of leopard-print satin pyjamas. I had no energy to shower and change.

My phone screen told of a world that was rapidly changing beyond our control. News footage showed scenes of once-thriving landmarks – Times Square, Piccadilly Circus, the Champs-Élysées, the Trevi Fountain and Sydney Harbour – now empty, barren, lifeless. That global shutdown was hitting closer to home, too; we had received our own stay-at-home orders in Geelong, Victoria. The sense of danger and crisis – not to mention the narrowing of horizons, of one's perspective, as we were forced to remain inside for most of the day – was overwhelming, to say the least.

For the first few days of lockdown, I looked outwards in any way possible: on the TV news to hear how the situation was evolving far and wide; through updates from my friends locally, interstate and internationally; and by endlessly scrolling through my social media feeds. There was a comfort in reminding myself that there was collective despair beyond my own.

The year before, I had moved back to my family home in Geelong after being made redundant from my dream job, one I had spent the better part of a decade working towards. I was thirty-one years old and had spent most of my twenties running away from the town I grew up in. I'd travelled and lived in bigger cities with brighter lights: Paris, London, Sydney. These cities made my wildest dreams come true, only to fall short on delivering a life and a sense of self that felt like truly my own.

After the initial lockdown shock made way for acceptance, I shifted my gaze from the world beyond to look deep inside myself, to the core of my identity. This was largely because of lockdown, though also partly because of my circumstances at that time: I was unemployed and had just signed up for Centrelink, had recently become single, and was back home with my parents. When your life suddenly becomes this stripped back, you listen deeply to yourself.

I was also negotiating another, even more personal change. Two months before, I had recognised for the first time what had always been my truth, what my inner child had always known but hadn't had the language to articulate – which was that I am non-binary. We'll get to this in more detail later, but suffice to say that this (re)discovery of my gender identity asked big questions of me during those early weeks of lockdown: *What does it all mean? Who am I? What am I doing with my life?*

Why was I so afraid to step into my truth?

It would take one redundancy, the most formative breakup of my life, coming home to regional Victoria and a global pandemic for me to finally turn the light switch on.

Light switch? you ask.

Bear with me.

Hello darlings, my name is Deni. My pronouns are they/them. I identify as non-binary, Queer and gay. I am an Aries, born on the first of April in Geelong, Victoria, Australia. I'm a brown human living in a very white world. Born to migrant parents, who came here to the 'lucky country', my ethnicity is Serbian-Romanian with an ancestry that I've recently discovered began far beyond the Balkan region – but more on that later too.

I wasn't born Deni, however, nor was I given they/them pronouns at birth. I was born Ratko Denis Todorović, the first son of Zlatko and Maca Todorović. I was assigned male at birth, given he/him pronouns and assumed to be heterosexual.

Those of you reading who follow me on Instagram @stylebydeni will be familiar with my trajectory thus far. For those of you who don't and have picked this book up because you (hopefully) like the sound of what it could offer you, let me clue you in.

I have spent almost thirteen years working in the fashion and media industries. My career has spanned roles including public relations, marketing, buying, trend-forecasting, celebrity styling, fashion styling, fashion blogging, fashion editing, video editing, picture editing, journalism, podcast hosting and content creation. Whadda mouthful!

Alongside each of these roles, my work has been grounded firmly in two lanes: storytelling and psychology. Psychology is the single greatest aspect of my day-to-day work, and it's no overstatement to say that all of the previous circumstances and actions in our lives accounts for each decision we make.

Whether it's as simple as buying the perfect mascara (which, by the way, is really hard to find) or deciding whether or not to finally leave your cheating boyfriend (even harder), every single decision is a result of the way your psyche has been formed, over the course of your life and often by other people. A huge part of my job is tapping into authentic ways to connect with my audience on a deep psychological level and, crikey, do we go deep.

There is one recurring theme in the daily messages I receive. They almost always read along these lines: 'Deni, how is it that you are so confident? How do you love yourself the way you do? How have you managed to live such an authentic life? Can you teach me to be like that?'

Every time I read those messages my heart sinks a little deeper, and then my next instinctive feeling is to provide solutions. I'm a solutions-driven human. While no single person has the power to fix another (trust me, I've tried), as siblings of humanity we can all offer support and safe spaces for healing.

So with that, my darlings, this book is born.

I believe that life is a sum of many sliding-doors and crossroads moments that provide great lessons and evolution, if you're willing to listen. It is in those moments we either make our way towards the light or walk away from it. When you dig a little deeper, you'll find that this proverbial 'light switch' we're all so desperately searching for is defined by the need to discover our authentic identity.

What does it mean to live authentically? Beyond the buzzword that has made its way front and centre of many a social movement and ad campaign, some I've even fronted, living authentically at its core is a very simple concept.

I want you to think back to your child self. Anyone who has done any kind of trauma healing or therapy will be familiar with the premise that, in order to truly heal from trauma, one must make peace and reconnect with their inner child. When I think of true authenticity, I often think of young children. Without a care in the world, without knowledge or understanding of the many obstacles they are presented with, they simply live and exist, in the flow of what feels right to them, in the moment.

This is why so many of us look back fondly on our childhoods. As kids we were too young to fathom judgement for the way we looked, or identified, or for the things we loved and which brought us joy. An AMAB child steps into their mother's heels because it's fun and sparks joy; it isn't until an adult tells them not to that they are instilled with self-doubt. So the seeds are sown for deep-rooted stigma and trauma to manifest in our adult lives.

It's something I see a lot of, both in my own life and in members of my online community. I have conversations with many individuals who feel as though they are running through life on autopilot, stuck in ruts of all kinds, conforming to rules even when they no longer serve them.

While many people find themselves feeling this way, I see this crisis especially among cishet (cisgender and heterosexual) women in their thirties and beyond, because, duh, the fucking patriarchy. These women have followed scripts presented to them by society, government or religion, some by their families and others by way of comparing themselves to the women around them or the ones they follow on Instagram. Often these scripts for career, marriage and kids never felt completely authentic to them, and they feel let down by the life options available to them.

I see this crisis also in my mother, and women of both her generation and background, who feel as though it's 'just too late' to start over again.

I see it in Queer people who haven't yet found their community, who hold back from showing the world who they really are or, worse still, don't allow themselves to feel who they authentically are.

I see it in young people who are still trying on different versions of themselves and seeing which ones fit.

I see it daily: humans of all identities going through life with their light switch off. Some never to turn it on.

The moment I turned my light switch on, my life changed forever. If 2020 was the year in which I wrestled with big questions about my life, my career, my gender and my relationships, 2021 was the year in which I started to manifest and realise a life that exceeded even my own expectations of what could be possible. I had come out as non-binary, to my family and friends and to my followers, and after that, so many things started to fall into place.

In 2021 I was the face of the Self Love Uprising campaign for iconic beauty brand The Body Shop. I had been out as non-binary for less than six months at the time of shooting the campaign, and I'd just appeared on the cover of a Geelong magazine telling my coming-out story. Although this catapulting into the public eye wasn't an overnight turn of events, given I'd worked in fashion media and journalism for more than a decade, I was proud of becoming somewhat of a 'poster they' for activism, even though I initially struggled with impostor syndrome. I settled on this reading of the situation: this was the universe's way of telling me that, in this very moment in time, I was exactly where I was meant to be.

When a billboard-sized image of you appears alongside the words SELF LOVE all over the country, people start to associate you with this movement. I started to reflect on all the questions that have made their way into this book, and most importantly, what it means to lead an authentic life.

Authentic living means being true to one's core self, unapologetically without fear of judgement. It can be a lifelong journey, but a journey worth enduring.

Over the next ten chapters I'm going to take you on the start of this journey.

YOU'RE ABOUT TO FALL DEEPLY IN LOVE WITH YOURSELF.

I know that sounds like a self-help slogan, but I promise you this is not a self-help book. Rather, I want you to think of this as a guidebook, the destination being your authentic self.

This book is filled with stories and lessons. The lessons I've learned. The mistakes I've made. Believe me when I tell you,

I've made ALL the mistakes. Every single one. But somewhere along the journey I learned more than I could have ever possibly bargained for.

That said, this book is also not a memoir – I have more life to live before I write that one. My life lessons are here to guide you through the work I've done so that you, darling, can start your own.

Each chapter corresponds to the key life pillars that I believe to be the foundations upon which a person's identity is built. We'll start at the beginning, as children, and move our way through the universal crossroads moments that every human faces. No matter how you identify or what your lived experience, there is a selection of universal truths we all encounter, from family dynamics to culture, religion and faith. Through to our often awkward teenage lives, high school, hormones and puberty, sex and sexuality. We'll travel through our work lives together and the moves we make in order to find ourselves professionally. Some of these crossroads moments will ring more true than others, and perhaps it'll be within those gaps that you find you've missed the various fundamental rites of passage to truly discovering who you are at your core.

Each 'life pillar' is chaptered by way of a piece of clothing that symbolises a particular season of my life to date, and the crossroads moment in which I made a decision to change things up and live more authentically. Fashion was always going to be a part of this book, given the important role that clothing plays in telling the story of all our of our lives, and certainly the way it has in mine.

Within each chapter, I'll talk you through the lessons learned. There'll be a tonne of advice, homework for you to do and solutions that I've road-tested and which actually work.

Each chapter has a takeaway that comprises calls to action and moments of introspection so that you, as you make your way through these pages, begin to undertake the necessary work to inch yourself closer to your authentic self. Examining the 'rules' so that you, too, can rewrite your own.

Then it's over to you, darling, because once you've taken yourself back through the sliding-doors moments of your own life, the real work begins.

I should mention that there'll also be dance breaks, because dancing is a cure for the soul. There'll be playlists for each chapter, because music is the blood that runs through my veins. There are codes for you to scan at the end of each chapter that'll take you to a playlist I've curated for you to make our dance breaks effortless. There'll also be pop culture history and some expert advice, because no one person has all the answers and this is an inclusive gathering – OKURR!

Speaking of expert advice, we have a secondary voice guiding us through the body of this book. Her name is Elise Condon and I would love you to think of her as our oracle, offering wisdom and spiritual insight when we need it most. Elise is a healer, in both the psychological and spiritual space. Her healing practices have changed my life insurmountably, and if spirituality isn't your jam, she has psych credentials to back up her expertise in this space. Elise's Bachelor in Psychology and over twenty years of experience working in healing and psychotherapy has led her to become a trauma specialist. She worked for the Royal Commission into Institutional Responses to Child Sexual Abuse, and also with not-for-profit agencies helping children and families who have endured traumatic experiences to reclaim their confidence and connection to a safer world.

I was referred to Elise by a dear friend during a particularly dark period of my own identity journey, and it was Elise who saw something inside of me that sparked the beginning of the rest of my life. As dramatic as that may sound, I often wonder what would have happened had I not found myself on the couch of Elise's office in the presence of her warm energy, admiring through my sadness the curl in her hair, her eyes piercing right through my soul. Elise guided me to my authentic self in more ways than I could likely express, so it is my great privilege to share her voice and insights here with you.

I should also give you the heads-up and a content warning that there will be swearing, themes of abuse, domestic violence, disordered eating and suicidal ideation, but all of these themes will be covered with the greatest level of care. There'll also be lists of organisations and numbers you can call in times of need.

Now that we're better acquainted, let me set the scene so you can feel the vibe, hun.

I'm sitting here in a pair of grey marle Bonds trackpants, wearing a bright green t-shirt from my merch range that reads 'Empathy, Love and Kindness' on the chest. On my feet I have hot-pink satin quilted Balenciaga slippers. I have a thing for bougie slippers. (Fun fact: North West has the same pair.)

I'm drinking a Moccona – don't @ me, I love instant coffee. I've just eaten two chocolate Pop-Tarts, my favourite snack. I'm currently listening to a playlist called 'Inspiring Instrumentals', and I am ready to write.

Are you ready to read? Go on, pour yourself a cuppa, put your slippers on, why not go crazy and put some Pop-Tarts in the toaster. I'll wait for you.

You back, doll?

Okay.

Now, before we dive in, can I just say a big bloody thank you for parting with your hard-earned cashola to buy this book. I understand the value of your dollar, so truly, darling, thank you.

I also want to cheer you on as you take this step towards your own gender identity. Stepping into one's authentic self means putting in the work, and your being here tells me you're ready to do it. That is something you should be proud of. Mazel tov, darling!

This book is my gift to you. It's the book I wish I had growing up. It's the book I wish I had every time I've felt lost – which is more times than I can count. So, as you settle in to read it, I want you to remember the following:

Life is not a dress rehearsal. You only get one stage call. One.

Make your way firmly to the centre; you've spent long enough over at stage left. You are the main character.

Are you ready? Of course you are, hun.

Let's go turn your fucking light on!

1.

Where it all began

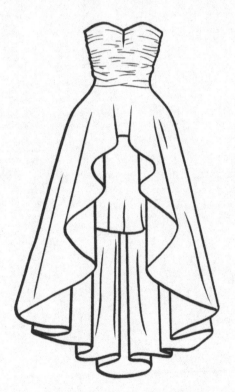

I was once told by a therapist that the most formative years of a person's life are from birth to age three. THREE.

What could a parent possibly do to their child aged zero to three to impact the course of their life? Most people don't even recall memories that far back. (I perhaps strangely do – but my wildly vivid, photographic memory is a subject for another time.) I found it hard to believe this fact at first, even though said therapist specialised in the psychology of family and domestic abuse. So, like the occasionally sceptical millennial that I am, I went to Google to do my own research.

Turns out he was right.

I came across a report released by the Victorian Department of Education and Training that highlights just how crucial those early years of life are in forming the ways we will learn and behave as kids and teenagers at school, and as adults in the years beyond. Some researchers use the term 'early years' to mean from birth to eight years; to others it means the years before school; and others, like my therapist, focus mainly on the first three years of life. However those formative years are measured, this is the period when the foundations for our future are laid.

I walked into the aforementioned therapist's office in the autumn of 2019. This was right after my redundancy, my breakup and return to Geelong. A big crossroads moment before I'd made that all-important decision in lockdown to turn on my light switch.

I'd gone to this specific therapy service – the brilliant Thorne Harbour Health (THH) in Melbourne, Australia's oldest and Victoria's largest LGBTQIA+ health organisation – by recommendation of a friend who works in the Queer health sector. This would be my third therapist in ten years, after a third failed relationship within the same timeframe.

Remember Anastacia, the early noughties pop singer with the epic growl in her voice and even more epic blue-lens sunnies? One of her songs speaks to her experience of feeling constantly sick and tired of someone's shit – so much so that you yourself become sick and tired of actually being sick and tired. Very that.

On that first day, I found myself feeling somewhat triggered by the category of therapy to which I'd been assigned by the induction counsellor at THH: family and domestic abuse. I even protested this with my therapist: 'I was raised in a really loving family. Aren't victims of abuse typically raised in abusive homes?'

He looked at me, then down at his paperwork and said, 'Deni, could you describe your family to me?'

'My parents are the best. They love unconditionally. The door is always open. Everyone is welcome. They greet you with a warm hug and there is always food on the table.'

'So there are no boundaries in your house, then?'

His response stopped me in my tracks. He repeated my statement back to me and broke it down line by line.

They love *without* condition.

Their door is *always* open.

Everybody is welcome.

They greet you with warmth and then proceed to *feed* you.

There are no boundaries in my family.

I had never thought about my family dynamic in that way, but he was absolutely right.

'This, Deni, is why you're here today. Because neither you nor your family have boundaries.'

I spent every Tuesday morning in that therapy chair, and for the next twelve weeks my therapist and I would unpack the many layers of my trauma. What I soon came to understand on a very visceral level was that every intersection of said trauma was linked back to my childhood. Internalised racism? Tick. Internalised Queerphobia? Tick. A pattern of attracting humans who need fixing? Tick. An innate desire to fix everything and everyone? Tick. Such a lack of self-love that I let any and everyone do with me whatever they choose? Tickiddy-fucking-tick.

So, let's take it back to the very start, shall we? To a purple, taffeta bridesmaid dress.

The purple dress was strapless, ruched, with layers that shot from the hip out. It was like a piece of fashion confectionery.

My mum wore the dress to my auntie's wedding, where she was maid of honour. Except that she was late to the ceremony and didn't get to sign the witness papers. Because my family are perpetually late to everything and run on their own time zone, I say we operate according to 'Todorović Time'. Because. No boundaries.

Anyway, I digress.

I was eighteen months old in the pictures Mum has of me at this wedding, sitting in her lap in a little white suit. When Mum would show me those pictures afterwards, I remember wishing I could have worn her dress.

Mum kept the dress in a white box, at the top of her closet. I could often see slivers of purple taffeta pushing out from its lid. I was four years old when one Saturday morning, while Mum and Dad were sleeping in, I did what any small Queer child would do. I'm not sure how I managed to find a stepladder but I did, then opened it, stood on my tiptoes and got the dress down from its treasured place in Mum's wardrobe. I took it with me into the living room and pulled it out of the box.

I will never forget how the dress felt in my hands. The sound of the poly-taffeta rustle in between my fingers. I also managed to take a pair of pointy-toed kitten heels from Mum's wardrobe to pair it with. Very quietly, I put the dress and heels on; both were way too big for me. I twirled around the living room, watching as the fabric danced around my body, for five glorious minutes. I took it all off. I put it all back.

Over the course of the next month I would do this every weekend, each week spending more time in the dress.

One weekend, I got my brother in on the game. My sweet brother Michael, eighteen months my junior, who would do anything I asked of him. He couldn't have been older than two, but he understood my instructions. I found a shirt from Dad's side of the wardrobe to dress him in, and we sat at opposite ends of the kitchen table. I had this grand idea that we would both play a character: me, this glamorous woman in her purple gown; my brother, her handsome husband in a white shirt. Our roaring giggles filled the living room.

I'll never forget what happened next.

My parents were standing at the door to their bedroom, which opened out into the living room. My mother yelled, 'What are you doing?' as my dad followed with a stern instruction: 'Deni, take that off.' This conversation took place in Serbian, as did most when I was that age. 'That's not for you,' Dad continued. Without saying the words 'dress' or 'boy', I knew exactly what he meant.

Dad held one of my hands in the air. The other met the dress on my body as he wriggled it down past the pyjamas I wore underneath. As I spun, crying, the dress came off me. It hit the floor, and my dad hit me.

Before you freak out, reader, I must tell you that in many ethnic cultures, children don't receive a 'time-out', nor are we told to sit in the naughty corner and think about our mistakes. You aren't given the agency to 'think about what you've done'; your parents simply tell you what you've done 'wrong'. Often, this manifests physically, as a slap across the bum, the back of a head, a light slap of the face – a slap that intends to convey tough love, but a slap nonetheless.

This slap from my dad was the first time I was punished for feminine behaviour, but it wouldn't be the last.

✦

Funnily enough, despite these rules around gendered behaviours, my parents took no issue with my love of fashion and all things glamour. While at times I'm sure it scared them, more often than not they encouraged it.

As a child I was surrounded by glamorous women. The kind who aren't glamorous by way of money but rather an innate sense of style. One of my favourite things to do as a kid was look at old photo albums, many of which were filled with snapshots of my mother, her sister and their cousins during the glory days of their nightclubbing era at the discos, as they were so affectionately called. Their outfits always stopping me in my tracks.

My mama would tell me stories of where each outfit came from. Some they made themselves, and others they saved their factory-job incomes for, to buy for special Saturday nights. Their aesthetic could be described as if Madonna, Culture Club and George Michael had a baby. Throw a little *Dynasty* in for good measure and you have peak eighties energy. It was the era of the New Romantics. Women blurred the lines of gender and tapped into themes of sexuality. Men wore make-up, grew their hair and sometimes wore Cuban heeled shoes. It was a time I dreamed of growing up in. A time, it seemed, when feminine behaviour in masc-presenting humans wasn't punished. How little I knew.

Another reason I became so interested in fashion was because I was raised by dressmakers. In the eighties my mother's uncles had migrated from Former Yugoslavia to Australia. One of them had three daughters, and upon moving to Australia, these women quickly dropped out of high school and entered the workforce. Noting their penchant for fashion, my uncle bought them industrial sewing machines and they would go on to work as seamstresses. He built them a shed in his backyard and I would spend much of my early life sitting in their shed, watching them sew.

Far from glamorous, their cutting tables mostly saw nothing more than tracksuits and the occasional t-shirt dress, but I didn't care. The whole process of making clothes enchanted me. My cousins gave me a safe space for exploration. I quickly learned that if you had an idea and someone to facilitate pattern-making and garment construction, your very own fashion fantasy could become a reality.

Week after week, I would sketch little outfits for them to make. First for my stuffed toys, then for me, each more elaborate than the one before. I was at the peak of an obsession with Madonna and Janet and Michael Jackson. Knowing that the first two were women and I was not, Michael became my main source of inspiration. (Let's bear in mind this was the early nineties, before we all became aware of how complex and problematic a figure Michael Jackson was.) I once went to a family function dressed head to toe in an outfit inspired by MJ's 'Beat It' music video. It was made from black denim and featured rivets and chains as far as the eye could see.

On another occasion I spotted a woman pass me at a set of traffic lights wearing a royal-blue velvet jacket. I ran to my cousin the next time we were at their house and exclaimed, 'I need a blue velvet suit.' Two weeks later, I wore that suit to a family dinner. I always knew exactly how I wanted to look, from the way my hair was cut down to the styling of my outfits. I got that from the many years spent sitting on my mother's bed watching her get ready for family functions and parties. Fashion, over a very quick period of time, would go on to become my armour. My great escape. My first true love.

Alongside fashion sat my love of performance. My mother would often say that I could dance and sing before I could walk and talk. The jury's still out as to whether or not I can *actually* sing, but dancing I can do. I grew up in the MTV era. I woke up every Saturday morning before anyone else in my house to watch *Video Hits* and *Rage* and record my favourite music videos on videotape, practising the choreography of my idols of the time. (For those of you too young to know what either of those shows were, they played music videos for up to four hours every Saturday morning, typically ending with a Top 10 countdown.) Mum recently told me that the only way she could get me to eat as a young child was while watching said videos.

Telly and movies? I was big on those too. My mum raised us on daytime soaps. Particularly *Days of Our Lives*, which she would set a timer to record daily and we would watch together as a family at night. The citizens of Salem seduced me with their drama-filled lives. The cast felt like an extension of my family and we watched the show every day, consecutively, for about seventeen years.

I couldn't get enough of films. From an early age I was perhaps most obsessed with the biopic genre, watching the real stories of larger-than-life celebrities like Tina Turner, Selena Quintanilla, Ritchie Valens and The Jacksons. There was something about their lives that spoke to me on a deep level: living their lives on stage. The bright lights. The adoring spectators. The shiny clothes. The glamour. The escape from small towns to big cities. It was everything to a wide-eyed, hopelessly romantic six-year-old. It's no coincidence that all of these singers also struggled with deep, complex childhood traumas. I was too young to understand the specifics, but what I did see were stories of great survival and bright fame, and I wanted in. I also realise now that those films told the life stories of people of colour, and as a little brown 'boy' in a very white town, these survivors became my heroes.

I danced at every moment I could, commanding the attention of a room full of adults, insisting they all sit down to watch me perform, much to their amusement. In Grade 5 my parents bought a really fancy video camera, the kind that weighed a tonne and required you to put an actual tape inside its case. I wrote film ideas down and shot them in the school holidays with my cousins. 'Deni's gonna be famous, you know?' was a sentence I heard people say to my parents a lot. 'He's not like the other kids.'

They were right about the second part. I wasn't like the other kids. Not even a bit. I had little to no interest in 'playing' with kids my age. They bored me. I preferred the company of my older cousins, aunties and uncles. I could sit, happily, at the dinner table while my relatives sat around gossiping, drinking whisky and smoking cigarettes, playing game after game of Monopoly until 3 am. Adult conversation intrigued me. I listened, always, soaking every story in, no matter how likely inappropriate it was for a kid to listen in on.

That was my childhood. My boundary-free childhood of deep obsession with glamour, fashion, celebrity and performance. It all seemed very innocent to me, until many years later, when I would learn in therapy once more that this pattern of performance had informed the course of my life, not always for good.

Let's refer back to the report by the Victorian Government on the influence of our early formative years on the people we will later become. I found it useful as a reference guide because it lists, in a systematic way, all the primary and secondary influences on our early years. According to this report, the primary influences on children's development and learning are:

- genetic inheritance
- gender

- temperament
- health.

Secondary influences include:

- family relationships
- parenting styles
- parents' financial situation
- parents' level of education
- parents' mental health
- parents' occupation.

And finally, to round it off, are the broader influences from the child's community and culture.

The reason I cite this report here is because it attempts to map an objective framework of sorts onto the complex, interrelated ways that nature and nurture shape us. Being able to compartmentalise the ever-evolving flow of our lives, to impose order on them, is a huge part of the work that serious therapy demands of us. We must all be encouraged, challenged even, to look back at our lives with a degree of emotional detachment, to figure out what has worked, is working and will work for us, and what must be left behind.

One way to think about this book is that, within each chapter, we'll perform an inventory of our lives, and the way our identities have been shaped by formative influences, in the same way that we often do an inventory of our wardrobes. Whenever I see that someone's wardrobe comprises one big, amorphous collection of clothes, it gives me anxiety. Shirts should belong with shirts, jackets and outerwear belong together, bottoms are organised according to hem length and style, and so on and so forth. When you have a wardrobe sectioned into compartments, it becomes easier to identify the gaps. The same organising principle should apply to your sense of self and your life path.

With that in mind, as our starting point, let's compartmentalise the following formative influences to determine how they've shaped the people we've become. I've based them according to some of the categories from the government report: family relationships; parenting styles; the financial situation, level of education, mental health and occupation of our parents; and influences from the child's community and culture. I'll provide a sketch of my own life next to each category, but I'd encourage you to start reflecting on your own as we make our way through.

Family relationships

I was raised in a very close, very big, loud, warm ethnic family, in a web of family relationships where everyone is in everyone else's business, where it is not solely the parents who raise their children but rather a village of family members. My grandparents were always over, my aunties and their daughters a close second. (Wogs never make appointments or call ahead, they just show up and knock. Our house was Grand Central Station.) When relatives came to visit they all did their bit, my cousins often bathing me, talking to me about the various stages of life they were in. My ears were always open, always present for these very mature conversations. My extended family parented me the way they saw fit, irrespective of my mother's opinion, much to her own disdain.

Parenting styles

In our house, parenting roles were pretty clear. My dad is a sensitive soul, very affectionate, a heart-on-his-sleeve kinda guy who could cry at the drop of a hat. It's one of my favourite things about him. He was the softer, in many ways more traditionally feminine parent, but also knew when he needed to lean into his strong authoritarian masc energy. When Dad told us off, we knew it was a big deal. Mum, on the other hand, was the tougher of the two, or at least that's what she'd like you to think. Deep down, she was more sensitive than my dad. What you see is what you get with my mother. If she likes you, you know about it and if she doesn't, you'll know too. I've always admired that about her. There was never any sugarcoating with Mum but there was always lots of sugar. Mum was great at keeping us entertained and often leaned into a beautiful childlike, playful spirit.

Parents' financial situation

I knew from an early age that my family wasn't rich. I didn't know what working class meant then but I do now, and that's how I would describe our place on the social ladder. I went to a very white, affluent public school. The mums would pick up their kids from school every day. Ours was at work in a factory, so we were babysat by our auntie. My mum would pick us up at 4.30 and then go home to cook us dinner. We often had takeaway. With this said, Mum and Dad would take us to the movies and we always ate from the candy bar. We were dressed beautifully and went on regular family camping trips. Looking back now, I don't know how they did it all with a combined salary of seven hundred dollars a week, but somehow they did. It's also worth noting my parents have always had a bit of a #YOLO approach to finances. Life's too short: buy the new car, build the new house, get the marble benchtop, go on that holiday, you deserve it – even if that means doing it on credit or refinancing your mortgage. This has been both a blessing and a curse, and something each member of my intimate family are very self-aware of.

Parents' level of education

Neither of my parents finished high school. Dad was drafted to the army, as was compulsory in Serbia at the time, and Mum dropped out after a couple of months of Year 9. Upon moving to Australia from Serbia, she and her sister endured such severe high school bullying – their peers weren't so kind to migrant students – that they begged their mum to put them straight into the workforce. Mum spent her teenage years working in factories across Geelong alongside her mother and sister. At eighteen she completed a secretary course in Melbourne (in the eighties, becoming a secretary was an aspirational career path many young women followed). My mum was quite studious and finished top of her class. The principal of her school put her forward for a reception job at a bank in Melbourne. But before agreeing to attend the interview, my mum called my grandmother to run the idea by her. Being the overprotective, over-attached ethnic mother that she is, my grandmother exclaimed, 'But you can't work in Melbourne, think of the travel, you live here in Geelong with us. Find a job here.' So my mum didn't sit the interview and would spend the next two decades of her life going from one labour-intensive factory job to another. She never forgave her mum for it. As such, Mum always encouraged my brother and me to follow our dreams and any path we wanted.

Mental health

I come from a family plagued with mental health struggles. Not that we knew to call it that growing up. There is a Serbian word, živce, that translates directly to 'nerves' in English. We had many family members who were 'sick in the nerves', as my mum would say. Both my grandmothers, their siblings, their parents, my mother and much later we would discover it affected my brother also. Poor mental health in my extended family often led to alcoholism, substance abuse, suicide attempts and in one case suicide. For a long time it was something I feared. I've watched mental illness, and the fear of it, control entire families and generations throughout our community. Part of this fear was because poor mental health was something to be ashamed of, so there was the double bind of illness and stigma to contend with.

Parents' occupation

My family are the hardest-working people I know. Our ancestors come from a long line of what I can best describe as carnies. Travellers who every summer would settle across various villages in Former Yugoslavia to set up 'shop' aka their tents and assemble carnival rides. It's how they made their living. My father especially worked centre 'stage' by his parents' side, over the carnival season, every summer for his entire adolescence. Alongside factory jobs, Mum and

Dad also worked on vegetable- and fruit-picking farms with my mum's father and stepmother. Our whole community did, and as such us kids would tag along most weekends to help our parents pick potatoes. The more bins we filled, the more our parents got paid, so they were onto something.

When I was a teenager, my parents would go on to own a commercial cleaning company, one that would see them reach economic highs and economic lows. For a very long time they juggled multiple jobs and have worked seven days a week almost exclusively for the last ten years. No matter how much money was or wasn't in their bank account, they've never lost their resilience and would go on to become the king and queen of reinvention. Skills I've acquired directly from them.

Community and culture

Ethnic people and Anglo people are, simply put, not the same. Like, not even slightly. This isn't to say that any one culture is superior to the other, but the differences are as clear as the sky is blue. The ethnic way is by no means the 'right way' – there's no such thing. It is, however, the only way I've ever known, and that's meant that while it's a positive influence on my life in many ways, unlearning its negative aspects has not come without difficulty.

So, my darling reader, I want you to reflect on your authentic child self. With childhood comes an innocence that's hard to replicate, and that means it's most often when we are at our most authentic. But with every passing year, and with the various layers of life experience and some trauma thrown in for good measure, we move further and further away from the child self.

Inner-child work is one of the key elements of trauma healing. We will talk about this at length over the course of this book, but I want you to take me as an example in order for you to start the long, hard work of self-analysis. Hold up a critical lens to your journey thus far. Which parts of your own identity are authentic versus how much have external influences informed the person you are right now?

Upon reading the above, I think you'd agree with this summary of child Deni:

Little Deni was a dreamer, obsessed with fashion, glamour, dance, music, pop culture and bright lights. They had an innate yearning to live a life on stage. They loved the ritual of sharing stories. They never fit into the 'boy' category society tried to push them into and wore dresses when no one was watching. They were reprimanded by society when their femininity shone through, but rather than resist it they continued to lean into it.

It makes me quite emotional when I reflect on the fact that now, aged thirty-four, I've arrived at a destination where I've never been closer to Little Deni. My dreams have come true. Those obsessions with fashion, glamour and pop culture now inform the ways in which I make a living. I live my life on the stage that is social media, and storytelling is my primary source of income. My femininity alongside my masculinity have fallen into place, and I no longer have to hide when I wear dresses and heels. I am, finally, at peace with my inner child. What I've come to realise is that Little Deni always knew who I was, what I liked and didn't like, what I wanted and didn't want. Little Deni knew exactly where I was going. I just had to catch up to them.

We are all too often dictated by the hands of society that push us in directions and categories we have no desire to go in. It's a tale as old as time. How many stories have you come across that speak to these themes of fear and rebellion? A parent hands down the family business to a child who has no desire to keep the business running. People enrol their children into the colleges they went to or, worse yet, the schools they never got a chance to attend due to their own lack of privilege, and so their children are left feeling as though they have to live out their parents' dream life. Humans the world over may feel stuck in unsupportive relationships because a partner has made them feel they have no other choice and just maybe they have mouths to feed. Have you ever made a decision based on how it would make you look in the eyes of those around you? You're not alone, darling.

Do me a favour, will you? Go grab a piece of blank paper. Fuck it, why not find yourself a notebook. I'll wait.

I want you to write the following down for me.

DESCRIBE CHILD **INSERT YOUR NAME HERE** IN A SENTENCE.

Let's do the following breakout sections. I want you to think way back to your childhood. Reflect on those crucial 'early years' and the dynamic with your immediate family (the humans who raised you, no matter whether they're biologically related to you or not). Now make notes. You could make dot points or write a short paragraph under each of these headings, like I just did for you.

Ready? Here are your headings …

Family relationships
Parenting styles
Parents' financial situation

Parents' level of education
Parents' occupation
Mental health
Community and culture

Then I want you to answer the following for me:

DESCRIBE, IN A SENTENCE, *INSERT YOUR NAME HERE* IN THE PRESENT TIME.

Now that you have this all on paper, the first thing I want you to do is compare your child self to your current self. Use these questions as your starting point:

- How close are you to that inner child today?
- What were your passions as a five-year-old? Have you let them go? If so, why?
- Are those passions in any way reflected in what you're doing with your life at present?
- If the answer is no, why do you think that might be?
- Did you like yourself as a child?
- Do you like yourself today?

It goes without saying that this, my darlings, is simply the beginning. But I promise I'm here to guide you, and before you know it there'll be a whole community of humans making their way through this book and we'll all be on the journey together. I'm your enby cheerleader in the sidelines, with fabulous bright pompoms and a cute lycra bodysuit, obviously.

Do you need a minute? I think you need a minute.

In fact, I'll give you four minutes and fifty-five seconds. You deserve a dance break (or in this case a sway break – you'll see) to let you ponder your first interactions with childhood trauma healing.

If you follow me on the 'gram, you'll know that I dance every single day. Dancing has always had a healing effect on me; it kept me sane during various lockdowns, and even now, most mornings you'll find me dancing in the kitchen as I make my first cup of coffee. This is why, at the end of each chapter, I will invite you to join me in dance: this is an immersive experience to break up the often heavy and introspective subject matter elsewhere.

 Dance break

To access the ready-made playlist I've created for this book, simply go into your Spotify app, go to Search, and click on the camera icon in the top-right corner. Use that to scan the code below, and you'll see the full playlist. We're going to go through these songs one (or a few) at a time as we make our way through each chapter.

If you don't have the Spotify app, simply type the following song into your preferred streaming provider:

'Fix You' – Coldplay
Now, before you press Play, a bit of music trivia for you: Did you know Chris Martin wrote this song for Gwyneth when her dad died? Heartbreaking, in the best kind of way.

I want you to replace the notion of mourning a loved one with mourning the ways in which you might've become separated from your inner child. Because if you have this book in your hands right now, chances are on some level we have to reconnect you with them.

Okay, now it's time for you to press Play. See you in a few minutes.

You back? Take three deep breaths in and out. Through the nose, out the mouth. Because guess what: those lights, darling – you'd better believe they're gonna guide you the fuck home.

… and you are going to fix YOU.

Not me, honey, not them, not anybody. YOU are.

A Christmas miracle

I'm going to end this chapter with a story, one that I hope will light up your insides. It's perhaps my favourite childhood memory, and proof in the proverbial pudding that even among trauma and discomfort, unconditional love always wins.

I started school a year earlier than was routine in Australia. I was four and a half. As a young child I could read and write at quite a mature level – thanks, Mum – and as such my parents wanted to get me into school. This also had something to do with the fact that my two favourite cousins/little best friends, Andrew and Danijela, were a year older than me and enrolling into primary school. Our mums liked the idea of us being in the same year level, so off we went to South Geelong Primary.

At the end of my first school year, 'prep' as we call it in Victoria, we had a Christmas concert. Our grade would be performing the

Nativity scene with the song 'Away in a Manger'. The boys were told to come dressed as shepherds, while the girls got to be angels. We didn't have a Jesus, Mary or a Joseph; just a very binary, rather boring scenario. The choreography could have been a little more elevated if I'm being honest, but that's neither here nor there.

Alas, upon this announcement I came home in floods of tears. I explained the dress code to Mum through heaving sobs: 'I want to be an angel like the girls, but my teacher said I'm not allowed to.' Mum kneeled down so that we were both at eye level. She wiped my tears away and said, 'Deni, if you want to be an angel, you are going to that concert as an angel. I don't care what your teacher says.'

She called my aunties, and what followed felt like a scene out of Cinderella. The next night there was a roll of white fabric sprawled out on the dining table, Mum's sewing machine and three Serbian women (Mum included) making me a white dress. Mum later took me to this gorgeous little shop, down what felt like a secret alleyway on Union Street in Geelong, and we bought a halo and some fairy wings.

The night of the Christmas concert came. Mama and I walked into the school hall proudly, hand in hand, with my dad, brother and my two aunties behind us. I was dressed in my full angel regalia. Category was: FUCK YOU, GENDER BINARY. MY SON WILL WEAR WHAT THEY WANT.

I don't remember whether we got any shameful looks. I'm sure we did. I don't even remember whether I got into trouble. What I do remember is that I was put centrestage.

I was elated; I felt like I was home. It was the first time I would stand at the centre of that very stage, breaking gender stereotypes – but it would most certainly not be the last.

Perhaps, even more vividly, I will never forget how it felt to see

Mum in the front row. Beaming smile, tears in her eyes, taking photos of me. I had made my family proud. The feeling was intoxicating and I would chase it forever more.

Alongside the fear, confusion and anger my parents occasionally displayed towards my femininity, there was more often than not a great amount of love and support for it too. My parents knew I wasn't like the other kids, and they would go on to become my strongest support system, though not without challenges of course. But I'd like to think their journey to allyship started right there, at that Christmas concert – because my mother wanted to affirm her child's identity, and no one was going to stop her.

 Affirmation

Affirmations are a powerful way to call out and declare things to the universe. If you're less spiritually inclined, they're a fabulous way to create more positive habits around the way we speak to ourselves. Leading with affirmative self-talk strengthens this connection between mind, body and spirit. We'll end each chapter with an affirmation that builds on the work we've been doing and acts as a palate cleanser before we move into the next.

My favourite way to practise these affirmations is by saying them out loud, three times in succession.

Repeat after me:

I love and honour you, my inner child.

*I hold space for you and make space for you, so that
you can walk alongside the present and future me.*

2.

It runs in the family

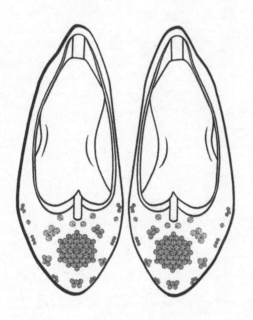

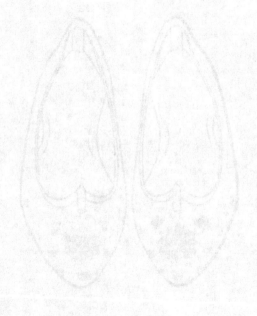

I've always had a penchant for a jazzy slipper, or really any kind of 'house shoe'. This is partly a result of growing up with parents obsessed with temperature control. (Right now, despite writing in the midst of a Melbourne heatwave, I'm wearing a pair of Versace slippers – black terry towelling, with the iconic Medusa logo embroidered across the front.) But this attitude is also an extension of the culture I grew up in. Ask any wog in Australia how their parents react to barefoot children and we'll all answer the same thing: 'What's wrong with you? Where are your slippers? Do you want to catch a cold?'

I remember being very little when I first fell in love with a pair of velvet amber-and-gold embellished slippers. My grandmother Rosa, who I now affectionately call Rose, used to keep them on display in a glass cabinet. Every ethnic family has this kind of cabinet. The kind that displays fancy plates and cups, seldom used, generally kept from 'the old country'. The kind that is only opened to clean the dust its contents has collected.

In my grandmother's cabinet there were crystal shot glasses, a dinner set, family photos and these heavenly embellished slippers. I'd beg my Baba Rosa to try them on, but they were ornament size. Big enough perhaps for a one-year-old, but far too small for four-year-old me. Even so, I tried every time to squeeze my foot into them, and then back in the cabinet they'd go.

Those little slippers, modelled off the traditional dancing shoe of Former Yugoslavia, represented home to me. No matter how old I got, whenever I went to my grandparents' house, after kissing them hello, my grandmother would typically make her way to the kitchen and offer me a Milo – tall glass, cold milk and two tablespoons thank you, served with a teaspoon so I could eat the crunchy chocolate bits – and I would inevitably make my way over to the cabinet to admire my favourite slippers. They were to me what red glitter heels were to Dorothy. A shining beacon of hope.

In Chapter 1 we looked at how crucial the 'early years' are, but here we're going to zero in on a particular category: family and culture. A huge subject that deserves a separate assessment. We're going to unpack how our families and cultures – used in the broadest and most inclusive sense possible – form our identity, no matter your background and no matter the colour of your skin.

As we continue on this journey of finding our true authentic selves, it's important for us to decipher the separation between child us and the us that was moulded and informed by our cultural context growing up – not only to understand the influence, its precise shape and power, but to also acknowledge how these influences might be difficult to fully escape. Often, without even realising it, the social codes and cues we pick up on as children are largely informed by our family's culture and, try as you may, you just cannot shake this way of being in the world. The older I get, the more of a middle-aged Serbian dad I become.

Ultimately, the aim of this chapter is to support you in making peace with who you are and where you come from, recognising what you can change and accepting what you can't, so that each of us can pave a clear, well-informed path for our present and towards our future. I also want to provide you with the freedom that I and so many others have given ourselves to create our own families and cultures: the chosen kind. I want us to look over the rules we've followed, throw them all out and then lean back into the ones of our choosing. Because, truth be told, no matter how much we rebel in our teens and twenties, more often than not, home really is where the slippers are.

Although my family had very little boundaries growing up, you should know that there was always an abundance of love, generosity and affection. I felt incredibly blessed by this element of my family's dynamic, long unaware that this wasn't necessarily the norm until I turned eighteen.

Upon graduating high school, I had to make a tough decision that many young humans face. University: to be or not to be? I'd never really felt academically inclined and wasn't sure that spending another four years in a classroom was what my soul needed, but I did want to further my fashion studies. But then, I also wanted to travel. Oh, to have these as my only two choices today!

I somehow found something that matched both of my desires: a fashion school, in Paris. I remember applying for the course and much of my extended family challenging my parents' 'decision' in 'letting' me travel halfway across the world to study. While most of my white counterparts were moving out of home, it became community gossip that I, an eighteen-year-old, should make my own decisions. I recall one relative saying, 'Fashion! Why? Deni won't make any money working in fashion.'

Despite the noise, my parents fully supported me. Only just. Mum did her very best to park her separation anxiety to the side and let her son get on a twenty-four-hour flight and spend a summer studying abroad. However, plagued by the memory of her mother not letting her take that job interview in Melbourne, she vowed to never stand in the way of her children's ambitions. My parents prepped my trip with great generosity, taking me to Melbourne to buy new luggage and to stock up on 'fashion school appropriate' clothes.

When it came time to bid me farewell, it was at the airport that I truly realised how the dynamic of my extended family differed from others.

Let me set the scene. It's worth noting here that I was travelling to Paris to study with my best friend. Her family escorted her to the airport with a sensible four-person squad: her parents, sister and our mutual best friend. My family, on the other hand, comprised a thirty-member squad. In fact, I remember greeting my bestie's mum with open arms and her thinking that my family behind me were just strangers at the departure terminal.

'Oh wait, these are all your relatives?' she asked.

'Yes, they've all come to say goodbye.'

Her response stopped me in my tracks. 'Wow, how beautiful. That's love.'

I spun around: my squad, alongside my parents and brother, included uncles and aunties and cousins and grandparents. When we went to say goodbye, we all hugged and kissed and cried. And when I say cry, I really mean sobbed. Heaving sobs, like that scene from *Love Actually*.

All of this had been the norm for me. Growing up in the late nineties and early noughties, my family welcomed many of our relatives arriving as migrants and refugees from Serbia in the same fashion. We'd all gather as a big group to greet our arrivals with open arms and would cap the night off at someone's house for drinks. If a family member was heading overseas for an extended period of time, we did the same. Cars full of my relatives would make the hour-and-a-half journey to Melbourne's Tullamarine airport to wish them farewell. There were always tears: happy, joy-filled tears, alongside the sadder kind. It was all I knew. Each time I became more proud, but it made me feel somewhat 'different'. Weren't all families like this?

The times I noticed the cultural divide most were in my mixed-race relationships. I've dated white boys almost exclusively throughout my life, and while I'm not here to throw shade at their family dynamics, the differences between ours were like chalk and cheese. My family were affectionate, deeply affectionate. My brother, no matter our age, always kisses me hello and goodbye. We tell each other we love one another on a daily basis, something Dad always instilled in our house. I speak with my mum multiple times a day. This was often perceived as 'too close' by some of my partners and even my friends. But affection, intimacy and generosity are the foundations my family have been built on from the moment I entered the world.

What I've come to realise is that this generosity can so often be misread and, worse, abused. Your generosity will be deemed 'too nice'. Your affection 'too affectionate' and your intimacy as 'too keen'. But how can being kind and taking an interest in someone be seen as a bad thing? I know now that these comments speak more to the people making them and their own family dynamics than me or my own.

For this reason and many more, understanding and unpacking your family dynamics not only benefits you, but will also support your journey to unpacking your identity at its core.

With that in mind, I wanted to dig deeper into this narrative in therapy. One too many a broken heart and moments of abuse had left me in a deep state of uncertainty about my self-worth, my identity, the ways in which I exist in relationships. Platonic, romantic and familial. I had so many questions that needed answers. Was I in fact 'too nice, too generous, too affectionate and too keen' – and if so, how, and more importantly, why? Here's where I landed with my therapist.

Too generous: came via the lack of boundaries in my family. Without boundaries, generosity becomes not only expected but also often abused. This was passed on to me by a father who had little to no boundaries in his own childhood and a mother who had too many.

Too nice: came from my intrinsic desire to please people. To be liked. To be seen. This came via a childhood of trauma, years of bullying and feeling like a perpetual outsider. Which to be honest summarises 'othering' in a nutshell. As with my generosity, this 'niceness' very much came via my dad, who, as the golden child in his family, adopted the nice nature in which he was spoken to and took it with him into his daily life.

Too keen: came via my own abandonment issues, which when we dug further came via a lack of self-love. For, if you do not love yourself and then find someone who loves you, you'd better believe you're doing everything in your power to try to make them stay. It was my lack of security and self-worth that saw me bend over backwards for every partner who had ever walked into my life. This aspect of my personality is once again taken from both sides of the coin, with Mum and Dad displaying signs of this in their own relationships.

Damn my parents and their ever-flowing, unconditional love – was a thought that crossed my mind often during therapy. But I also had to recognise that they, too, were products of their own complex family dynamics.

✦

You have one of two choices, my darling reader: to either mimic your family's patterns of behaviour or find other ways of doing things. I wanted to grow and evolve, choosing the best of each; my desire to never lose my generosity and kindness sat alongside one to become better at boundaries.

So let's get down to the intersectionalities of cultural trauma and intergenerational trauma, shall we? As much as your parents would hate to admit, all too often what was dealt to them is at some point dealt down to us. As in Chapter 1, to invite your own self-reflection on this subject, we're going to cover how I've seen it manifest in me and the people around me, in order for you to start to question how cultural trauma has affected you and your family dynamics.

For those of you for whom the subject of intergenerational trauma sounds quite overwhelming at first, let's start with a good old-fashioned Wikipedia definition:

Transgenerational trauma, or intergenerational trauma, is the psychological effects that the collective trauma experienced by a group of people has on subsequent generations in that group.

Take this example: one way that intergenerational trauma has manifested in my life stems its way back to my mother's childhood. Her feelings of unworthiness, the comparisons made between her skin and the skin of her classmates, her insecurities around her family's social class, were all, likely without her own realisation, passed down to little Grade 2 Deni. The Deni that went to a play date at the mansion of their rich white primary-school bestie and instantly felt as though they didn't belong there. No one taught me to feel that way, it was intuitive. The trauma sat somewhere in my subconscious, felt long before my time.

Now it's important to note that the above trauma manifests differently depending on your cultural background. A white person's intergenerational trauma will never be the same as that of a First Nations person or a person of colour (POC). This is because of white privilege – but more on that later.

Remember Elise, who I mentioned in the introduction, our psych-spiritual oracle guiding us through this book? When I broached this huge subject with Elise, one of her first observations was that, throughout her life's work, women in particular are impacted by cultural expectations, often feeling as though they are torn between what is expected of them as a mother or a woman or a wife within a cultural context and what might be expected of them within other contexts. The same can be said for Queer people and also for men – because no matter what culture you belong to, toxic masculinity edges its way in.

Going back to my mum, for example: she was raised largely by alcoholic uncles, and saw her and the women in her family made to play the roles of homemaker, the peacemaker, the subservient and often the silent. Her familial trauma saw much of her childhood taken away from her, as she witnessed firsthand the unreliable nature of the men in her life and had to grow up quickly. I think about the way in which both familial and cultural norms have dictated my own roles in life, in particular the limitations that gender stereotypes and cultural expectations have placed on my own decision-making.

Elise went on to explain that almost every POC who has ever sat on her couch has encountered childhood bullying and feelings of othering, whether it was that their hair was different, the colour of their skin, the food in their lunch box, the languages they spoke at home or the amount of money in their family's savings account. This category of bullying can take years to work through and, for some, is all too often left unresolved. When I think back to my childhood, the racist/cultural bullying my brother and I encountered in primary school on a regular basis almost always surpassed the homophobic kind thrown my way.

Another interesting point Elise made was that she found some women who were either children of migrants or migrants themselves recognised they felt a real disconnect to their origins later in life. They've had to assimilate and become more white to fit into the mostly white countries they've migrated to. Many refuse to speak their native tongue or refuse to learn it against their family's will.

This rhetoric is all too familiar to me. I grew up observing a handful of cousins and aunties who rejected their 'wogness'. These cousins refused to speak Serbian-Romanian and rudely spoke back to their Serbian-Romanian-speaking elders, 'Talk English, Baba, I don't understand you' – when the older relatives knew full well that they did. I've heard my cousins say things like, 'I'm Australian, my parents are Serbian', and I never quite understood why they rejected their identities so vehemently, and wondered what they were so ashamed of. Except that I knew. I knew it all too well.

My mum used to tell me stories of how, as a young girl, her mother tried to wash her brown skin away in the bath; the very notion that her skin made her inferior diminished her confidence and self-worth, one scrub at a time. These moments stick with us as individuals, so it's no wonder that they filter through intergenerationally. After all, in a white cishet world, it's the path of least resistance to fit in.

I've seen people change the spelling of their names, and their names altogether, undergo nose jobs and even speak with an 'Aussie' accent in order to try to assimilate to this white country. I used to cringe in my chair every time a substitute teacher tried to pronounce my birth name – which, as you now know, is Ratko. I spent years as a teenager cursing my big crooked 'wog nose' and my unibrow, which became hairier and more prominent by the day. It wasn't until I turned twenty-two that I finally grew into loving my nose, not till 2020 did I stop plucking and waxing my eyebrows and it wasn't until my grandfather of the same name died eight years ago that I felt proud of my first name. Cultural traumas, no matter how big or small, take time to work through. The reality is that sometimes they aren't healed at all.

But if you are reading this and you are *gasps* white – congratulations, you're in the majority. So how has intergenerational trauma impacted you, my darling?

Elise went on to explain how ignorance of white privilege can feed off, and in turn feed, the ignorant histories that have been taught for generations in Australia, which deny the fact that non-Indigenous people are living on stolen land. Because many white Australians don't feel connected to their cultural origins and ethnicity, or likely know little to nothing about said origins, this typically results in a lack of understanding of who 'you' are and where 'you' come from. If Australia is all you feel connected to, it's likely someone in your life still celebrates the genocide and invasion of January 26th and someone else in your life has at some point told someone who looks like me to 'go back to your own country'. If you identify with this description, I'm not here to shame you, darlin'; I'm here in the name of self-awareness.

If you looked up at the world, over at your television, or down at your phone at any point during May and June 2020, you will have watched the Black Lives Matter movement unfold. You would have learned (or relearned) some more, I hope, about the inequity in the world, of the racism that plagues every corner of the globe, and I hope you would have learned about the roles you play within it all. If you are a white person reading this, I would hope that two years on, you have an understanding of white privilege, systemic racism and implicit bias. If you do not, please put this book down for a moment and make your way over to YouTube. There is a plethora of videos and Ted Talks that will enlighten you.

If you are reading this and you are on the spectrum of colour, I'm sending you a big hug because, in my experience, people of colour are less likely to 'do the work' when it comes to being in therapy. There are many reasons that, statistically, there are more white people in therapy than there are any other race, but when I think about my own lived experience it is privilege that is the overarching factor. And the stats back this up: we know that racial and ethnic minorities have less access to mental health services than white people, they're less likely to receive care and, when they do, it's likely to be of poorer quality.

I've heard people around me say things like 'wogs don't go to therapy' and 'therapy is only for rich white people' more times than one would like. While I'm not here to be your therapist, the fact you are here speaks volumes to me of the internal work you're looking to do and the desire to reintroduce yourself to the authenticity you so clearly have.

Okay, Deni, so how do we unpack cultural trauma? I hear your question, loud and clear.

Elise's advice was very interesting to me, in that it was something my brother and I have sat down to do with our parents and grandparents more than once.

Step 1: Start with tracing through your origin story

Do your family tree, as far back as you can go. Note down any traumas that may have existed within said family tree. Get curious, ask questions about everything, from mental health to other kinds of illness to other forms of trauma.

I know this might sound grim, but it will honestly put so much into perspective. When my brother and I did this exercise many years ago, we learned that our great-grandfather was a Holocaust survivor, that mental illness seems to be hereditary on Mum's side and that I had a gay uncle who never came out. Alcoholism was evident in both sides of our family tree, as was infidelity and abuse. My dad even has a mystery, undiscovered, 'illegitimate' brother floating around somewhere in the world.

My family tree was full of collective trauma that has trickled through our identities. Having that on paper brings quite an unmatched clarity. For example, it was doing this investigation that brought my brother a sense of peace in reconciling with his own mental health struggles. To see so clearly and visually where we've come from and how that's played a part in making up who we are was really rewarding for us.

Step 2: Ask yourself the question: what happened before you were here and how has that impacted where you are today?

This is where we start to get intimate and perhaps even a little bit confronting. I want you to think about what the world was like when your parents were your age and then, following that, what the world was like growing up for your grandparents. What you'll find is that your environments were worlds apart. Our older relatives grew up without forms of modern technology, some without access to education, without autonomy over their bodies, different layers of choices, rights and identities. My parents for example existed at the time of the AIDS epidemic and their parents existed at a time when being Queer simply wasn't an option, nor was it legal. Our grandmothers may have existed in a time where they weren't afforded the right to vote. In some parts of the world, it may have been illegal for them to even drive a car. Can you imagine?

The reality is that the environment in which we were raised, alongside every single choice our parents made (or didn't make) in raising us, was a direct link to things that happened before we even arrived into this world. The same was done to them and the same to those who came before them. If you're reading this and you too are a parent or guardian, think about how your own environments have impacted the way in which you raise your children.

Were the choices you were given as a teenager informed by the toxic masculinity and strict gender roles placed on your parents, grandparents and beyond? Highly likely. Did you have to keep your abortion a secret because of a Catholic upbringing? Was your Queerness closeted for the same reasons? Were you made to feel like the duties of a woman are to cook and clean and raise children? Were you told to 'man up' at the sight of a single tear? Did religion riddle you with guilt every time you masturbated? Did you feel the impacts of racism as a child because of the colour of your skin? Have you ever been put on a diet by your parents?

We're starting to get a sense for what this big, scary subject of intergenerational trauma means in practice.

Step 3: It's time to unpack and start healing

To introduce this step I want to share with you a quote that never fails to take my breath away.

Let me start from the beginning. It was 2002 and Greek-American comedian Nia Vardalos took the world by storm with the film based on her life story, *My Big Fat Greek Wedding*. My cousins and I made our way to our local cinema and piled into the theatre to watch the movie.

If you haven't seen the movie yet, what are you doing with your life? (No, it's okay, I forgive you.) In a nutshell, it centres on the life of Toula Portokalos, a thirty-year-old Greek-American waitress, working for her parents' family business. Toula feels trapped in the cage that is her family, her culture and their expectations, and she is also single. At thirty. A foreign concept to any ethnic parents.

In a bid to seek more out of life, she enrols into college, framing the decision as being 'beneficial' for the family business. She starts to dress differently, and takes a sandwich to school instead of moussaka. She also falls in love with Ian Miller, an Anglo-American from the 'right side of the tracks', whose stiff upper-lip upbringing is completely different to Toula and her family. In case the title didn't give it away, Toula and Ian are to be married.

The film is essentially about carving out your own independence and autonomy in an environment and culture that have never truly encouraged you to do so. *My Big Fat Greek Wedding* depicts ethnic families, the differences between ethnic and Anglo family dynamics and intergenerational trauma with sharp, piercing accuracy.

A week later we all piled back into the cinema to watch it again, this time with our parents in tow. Off we went, twenty of us. When I tell you the cinema was filled with roars, coming mostly from our seats, I mean it. Our parents laughed with such vigour they cried and subsequently, so did we.

There are two things I'll never forget.

The first was a comment the white women in front of us made. As the credits began rolling, I heard her say to the other, 'We'll have to make sure our daughters marry Greek boys. They're so much more fun and interesting than we are.' It was my first introduction to the fetishisation that often comes with white people dating outside their spectrum of colour, or lack thereof – but that's a conversation for another time.

The second thing that was burnt in my mind was a quote from the film. The beauty of Toula's spirit is that it becomes infectious and inspires many of the young adults around her, most notably her brother Nicky. During a difficult crossroads moment in which Toula is trying to reconcile her culture in the present and the intergenerational trauma of her family's past, which has very much informed their present, Nicky gives her some sage advice:

'Toula. Don't let your past dictate who you are, but let it be part of who you will become.'

I could cry just thinking about the impact of those words.

With great healing comes great acceptance, and as I told you at the start of this chapter, there are just some parts of you that you can never run away from. As much as I tried to adopt the 'modern', liberal 'Aussie' mindset the white humans around me had, I will forever be a big fat wog on the inside. AND THAT'S OKAY. In fact, it's bloody beautiful. The quicker I made peace with my cultural identity and understood better my family's past and our intergenerational traumas, the easier it became to not let it dictate me, but rather let it play its part in my own becoming.

This work allowed me to choose freely the parts of my cultural identity and family dynamics I loved so dearly and combine them with the chosen family I had created and new cultures I had experienced throughout the course of my life. Among my Queer chosen family, I've learned to take the rulebook and throw it completely out the window. Dismantle and rebuild. Erase and rewrite. Blood isn't always thicker than water and biology only gets you so far. My Queer chosen family have shown, by example, that love really is love. They've taught me to marvel in community. To celebrate uncelebrated wins. To amplify voices all too often silenced. Over the years I've come to realise that, whether we're gathered in a living room watching *RuPaul's Drag Race*, drinking Long Island iced teas at Stonewall, dancing at Poof Doof or exchanging sex stories at Little Congwong Beach, family gatherings need not look one and the same.

My Jewish friends have, over the years, reminded me of the beauty of both resilience and pause. At many shabbat dinners without our phones, we've used time together to honour rituals, custom and tradition, faith and family, while also holding space to honour those who faced great persecution before us.

My 'white friends' and their families have taught me a bunch over the years too. They've taught me a lot about boundaries. About respecting the choices of those around you rather than instinctively questioning them. They've taught me that talking about weight at the dinner table is really not a vibe, that B.Y.O. is kind of a genius concept and shouldn't be frowned upon and that when your child's door is closed, please knock before entering.

Crafting my own culture, my own familial codes and the nuances of how I would like my family to feel has been one of the single most rewarding experiences of my adult life. Combining the old with the new. The familiar with the foreign. The 'biological' with the 'chosen'. All beginning with healing and great acceptance.

Might I also suggest therapy. I can't even tell you how both psychological and spiritual healing have helped me unpack the above traumas. Just ask Elise, she has the receipts.

With the final step in this chapter, I want you to make way for healing.

Over to you, darling

I want you to write yourself a letter. Now that you've done this work on your family tree and dug around a bit more into your family history, list all the elements of cultural and familial trauma that have impacted your life, from the environmental to the biological. Make peace with those factors, release the ones that don't serve you and make room for the ones that do. Create space to celebrate the many nuances that made you who you are – the smelly salami sandwiches, the accent in which your parents speak, the colour of your skin and the texture of your hair. Or the Vegemite on toast, the sneakers in the house or being barefoot at Coles. All of it is you and all of it is beautiful.

Let me help you get started – try starting your letter as follows:

To my child self,
I write to you today from the future. My intention is to make peace with our past in order to find our way to a clearer present and future.

Then get a bit more specific. Zoom in on three specific memories about your family or culture growing up that represent moments of conflict and/or resolution. I want you to write down why/how those memories are significant, both at the time and in the present day.

If you're stuck, try these questions below as a starting point:

1. How has culture informed your family dynamic?
2. Did you feel the presence or absence of culture in your house?
3. How has your culture informed your sense of who you were growing up, and your sense of who you are now?
4. Is your cultural identity something you embrace or reject?
5. Do you feel connected or disconnected to your culture?
6. What are some ways that you can reconnect with your culture or create some space between your identity and its influence?
7. Is your cultural identity something that you're proud of?
8. Has your culture come with privilege or social inequity?
9. Has intergenerational trauma informed your identity and, if so, how?
10. How would you like to make peace with your cultural identity and trauma so that it can positively manifest the ways in which you live?

I think you've earned a dance break. This time I'm gifting you with the journey of two songs, to take you on a fitting emotional roller-coaster. Get ready to scan your Spotify code and make your way over to our playlist ...

Dance break

'Family Portrait' – Pink
We're gonna start here. I'll never forget this song coming out and my mum sobbing at every lyric, feeling that it in so many ways summed up her childhood. If your family dynamic was less than picture perfect, you're not alone and this song is the perfect anthem for you to belt some of that rage out.

'Family Affair' – Mary J. Blige
Now it's time to leave our situations at the door and shake our ass on the proverbial dance floor. This is the perfect song to capture this vibe shift, and you'll be better for it. Press Play.

Home is where the slippers are

To end this chapter, we'll revisit the slipper story we began with. For the slippers that I spent my childhood in love with would go on to teach me an invaluable lesson.

My obsession with those velvet, embellished, spectacular amber slippers only grew as I entered adolescence and early adulthood. There we would be, in Baba's dining room, Baba fixing me my glass of Milo, which later turned into a cup of coffee, in the kitchen, while I held the slippers from her glass cabinet in my hands.

'Baba, just so you know, when you die, you don't need to leave me any money at all, I don't need anything big or grand. All I want, as a gift from you, are these slippers.'

Every time I said that, Baba would laugh. 'I have no money to give you, my darling, so you can have the slippers, don't worry.' It was our little bit, we played it out often. Especially whenever we needed a laugh.

At the age of twenty-six, I found myself moving from Geelong to Sydney, with my long-term partner at the time. My grandparents have always lived a very humble life and over the years any time they've placed a sneaky fifty-dollar bill in the palm of my hand, I've accepted it knowing how much it meant to them. So as we made our rounds to say goodbye to my various family members before our departure, something very special happened when I went to say farewell to my Baba Rosa. After a cup of coffee and a slice of cake, she placed a box in my hands. 'Now, it's nothing big or fancy, Deni, but it's something from me to you. I want you to keep this with you wherever you find yourself living. So that you can have a piece of Baba, always by your side.' I knew what the box contained before I removed the last piece of sticky tape from the beautifully wrapped box.

As I saw the first sliver of amber velvet and glimmer of a gold bead, I burst into tears. Baba put her hands on my shoulders and simply said, 'You don't have to wait for me to die to have these, my darling. Take good care of them.'

As soon as my partner and I moved into our terribly overpriced Potts Point studio apartment, Baba's slippers were among the first things I put on display. They sat alongside more modern pieces of furniture, fashion books and designer candles. Their humble origins were a juxtaposition to my new shiny Sydney life.

I lived in that studio apartment for almost two years. A lot went down in those walls, huge amounts of change, discomfort, trauma, growth and evolution. However, those slippers were my constant. They would go on to serve as a reminder that no matter where I was, which country or state I lived in, who I was sleeping next to, what the colour of their skin was, which job I had, how much I weighed or how much money was in my bank account – home was where the slippers were. As long as they were with me, home would live forever inside of me and me alone.

 Affirmation

I make peace with my past.
I make peace with my culture.
I make peace with my family.

I honour all of this, and allow it to move me with power
in the present and into my future.

3.

The uniforms that bound us

I remember two distinct times, early in life, where I felt as though society had boxed me into a uniform I had no desire to be draped in. The first time was around the age of eleven. Category was: Christian Church realness.

I was ten when my parents started studying the Jehovah's Witness faith and nearly eleven when they were baptised – or, in layman's terms, officially began 'going steady' with old mate upstairs, the God we call Jehovah. Most Christian churches have an unspoken dress code: men wear suits with trousers and women wear modest dresses or skirts, ideally below knee length. Should you veer away from this dress code, I can assure you that you'll know about it.

As a child, I had no real issue with suits, I actually thought them to be quite beautiful. I still do. But I envied the women at my church in their feminine skirts, flowing dresses and high heels. Three times a week my family attended church. We attended Bible study on Tuesdays and Thursdays, and what can only be described as more of a formal sermon-type service on Sunday. This is all to say that, for close to ten years of my life, I put on a full suit three times a week. I'm talking blazer jacket, trousers, collared shirt and tie, henny!

Alongside our church rituals, bigger religious events also took place multiple times a year. We called them 'conventions', at which we would gather for a weekend filled to the brim with sermons based on the word of God. Some people would be baptised, too; I'm talking grown adults mostly, teenagers occasionally, submerged in front of a crowd of hundreds – sometimes thousands – of people, as they declared their commitment to Jehovah forevermore. (I mean, talk about conformity.)

The conventions were split into a hierarchy of categories. There were the district conventions, which were more local; the national conventions, which took place annually; and the international conventions, which would take place in much larger venues like Rod Laver Arena or the Sydney Olympic Stadium.

The more important the JW convention, the more effort you put into your outfit. Given my family were ethnic people who took great pride in their appearance, you could be sure that for every big convention, a shopping trip would ensue.

When I was eleven years old my parents wanted to buy my brother and me new suits for the national convention coming up. As smaller humans, vertically challenged if you will, it was very hard to find suiting that fit us, but we heard through another Witness that Footscray was where it was at when it came to suit shopping.

Now, anyone reading this based in Melbourne will know that over the last few years Footscray has become an incredibly gentrified, almost hipster 'burb in the western suburbs. But in the late nineties and early noughties, it was a truly authentic and gritty melting pot of Asian diaspora cultures. Largely a community of Vietnamese and Chinese folks who have blessed the neighbourhood with incredible markets, herbal medicine, beauty salons and SUIT STORES. Visiting Footscray for a day of suit shopping would later go on to become one of our favourite family rituals, something we would typically do twice a year.

On this occasion, our first pilgrimage to Footscray, my dad told us to pick out special suits for the convention. When you wear a suit three times a week, it becomes crucial to have a range of choices, otherwise that shit gets pretty boring. So on this occasion, after having mostly worn a boring black suit to church for an entire year, I was on the lookout for something different.

I think we spent almost three hours walking in and out of suit stores until we found 'the one'. I remember the moment vividly. We walked into what was a very small store that couldn't have been bigger than a master bedroom and was covered from floor to ceiling in suits. Three levels deep.

'The Suit' hung on a padded hanger in the 'kids/teen' section. It had three buttons. It was single-breasted and made of a microfibre blend. Microfibre was the height of suiting luxury at the time, don't ya know, and always more expensive than a poly blend. My dad, being the glutton for quality that he is, FROTHED at a microfibre suit. But what struck me most was its colour. BURGUNDY. I'm talking like a deep red-wine burgundy, honey. In a sea of blacks, charcoals and navys, this suit was to be my beacon of nonconformity.

'Tata, I want to try that one,' I said, pointing up at it.

'It's very different,' everyone exclaimed.

'I know, that's why I like it,' was my response.

Ever the supportive parent, my dad told the vendor and the man brought this precious beacon down with his 'suit stick' from the top row for little me to try. I made my way into the fitting room, which was essentially a mat on the floor, a rod and a curtain, and was just big enough to fit me.

I put on the suit and could feel myself instantly stand taller. It was perfect. When I stepped out, oohs and aahs filled the store from everyone involved. I wanted the overall look to be somewhat tonal and, as if reading my mind, the store owner suggested I pair it with a soft pink shirt and a burgundy tie matching the colour and fabric of the suit itself. It felt like a fashion moment. It felt like, well, me.

The truth is, every store we walked into typically had a women's section far more colourful than the men's. I was drawn to the colours in the women's department and to the colours of vibrant Footscray more generally, which were in stark contrast to overwhelmingly white Geelong. So if a suit is what society was going to put me in, then you better believe it was going to be on my terms and in one helluva colour.

Before I knew it, the store owner dropped to his feet to pin my alterations together and in an hour we were back, paying for the suit to return home with me.

The night before the convention, my mum steamed my outfit and I went to bed, reeling with excitement. The morning finally came and I sprung out of bed and put that baby on. Both my parents made a point to tell me how beautiful I looked as we got in the car. I felt as full of pride as I imagine a peacock must feel when it erects those fabulous fucking feathers. Until we arrived at the convention hall.

My family is always late but, for whatever reason, on this brisk Saturday morning we were five minutes early. As we made our way into the foyer, an older male cousin of mine made a point of saying that my suit was a 'girly colour'. I pretended not to let it get to me and sped up to find my mother's hand to hold. At lunch, an older female member of our church mentioned that my suit was 'very different', and another noted it was a 'brave colour choice'. How a colour could be seen as gendered, or 'different' or 'brave', was beyond me. Yet here I was, an eleven-year-old, leaning into nonconformity once more.

The second uniform that policed my adherence to social codes was the high school uniform. I went to a public school and my uniform consisted of grey wool trousers or shorts. For tops, we were given a sky-blue collared shirt and a navy-blue wool jumper. If you were a fancy kid, your parents could afford the school's heavy wool blazer. I always wanted the blazer, though from memory only the 'geeks' wore blazers. See: more categories.

The girls got to wear kilts – long, fabulous kilts that they would later go on to hem short, often resulting in detention. They also got to wear dresses, but this time I was less interested in those. It was the kilts I had my eyes on, the kilts I longed to wear. Instead, I wore a blue shirt, that goddamn navy jumper and those godforsaken trousers every single day for six years, no matter the weather. I couldn't wear the shorts, because in PE class the white boys made fun of me for having hair on my legs. 'Hairy wog' was a term I would go on to hear for the duration of my high school existence.

When I tell you high school was one long chapter of trying to duck and weave between the dance of conforming or not, I mean it.

I feel like most teenagers enter the first year of high school with a desire to fit right in. Slip under the radar even. Was that your vibe? I can assure you, darling reader, it wasn't mine. No, Little Deni over here, the same Deni who grew up OBSESSED with American high school rom-coms and dramedies alike, wanted their high school experience to be just like those movies. Particularly the musicals: big. Shiny. Highly choreographed. I expected my first day of high school to mimic the opening credits of *Grease 2* (if you don't know, the second movie is so much better than the first in every sense of the word and I will die on that hill). I've always been a bit disappointed with how lacklustre the Australian high school experience is, and I tried to make up for the lack of Hollywood production values.

In Year 7, it was announced at assembly that there was to be a school-wide talent quest. It was held annually in the hall, during the lunch hour. I don't remember what the prize was but I do remember my eyes lighting up when I heard about it. This was my moment to shine.

The year was 2000 and Destiny's Child had just released 'Say My Name'. It was the birth of my lifelong obsession with Beyoncé and I knew this was THE SONG. I enlisted two of my girlfriends to be my backup dancers and I choreographed the whole song for us, mimicking the music video. I was Beyoncé. It pains me to say this, but not only was the plan for me to dance in front of my whole school, I was also to sing. Now there are a few things to note here:

- I come from a very musical family. I'm talking instrument players and singers alike. In fact, my dad's uncle was for a time a recording artist in Serbia with a hit album. Music and entertainment very much runs through my DNA.
- As a child, I used to sing a lot. I would 'write songs'. I even put together a band, featuring my brother and

two cousins, and we used to record our voices into this boom-box machine. WILD. We were called 'The Wishes'. I was the lead singer, songwriter and generally the only band member who gave a fuck. We broke up pretty quickly.

- My parents always told me I had a beautiful voice. I wish you could see me roll my eyes as I write this.
- While I may be able to at times hold a note, I AM NOT A SINGER.

I repeat. I am NOT a singer.

Imagine me, the non-singer, getting up in front of a full high school hall to sing an R'n'B song that requires dancing and breathwork. Me, a penis owner, performing a song by a 'girl group'. This could only go two ways. People would think I'm iconic. Or I would be bullied every day for the rest of the year and every year thereafter.

I can assure you that it was the latter. For months, wherever I went, that song followed me. In line for the canteen. Walking past the bus stop. On the downball courts. In maths class. In home room. You get it. 'Say my name, say my name', they'd say, before roaring into laughter. They'd point at me and say, 'Aren't you that "gaybo" who sung at the talent quest?' Trying desperately not to internalise the disapproval of my entire school, I shrugged them off. Brushing off each comment, no matter how much it dug at my inner core. You would think that an entire year of being bullied as the gay kid who sung at the talent quest would scare me off for life.

You'd be wrong.

Two years later I hopped right back up onto that stage and SUNG once more, this time choosing possibly one of the hardest ballads of all time. I'd practised it for weeks. In my bedroom. In the drama hall. To my music teacher. To my parents. To my friends. I even bought the backing track from a local music store so I could sing it properly and in key. Except that when the day came and I gave the music engineer the backing track, it didn't work.

'What do you mean it doesn't work?'

'Your backing track doesn't work. Sorry, you mightn't be able to perform.'

Like hell I wasn't.

Before it was my turn to go on stage, the host of the talent quest asked me what I'd be doing.

'I'm going to be performing acapella today because the backing track isn't working,' I said confidently.

'Go for it, hun. What are you singing?'

'"Hero".'

'Oh cool, by Enrique?'

'Um no. By Mariah Carey.'

'You're singing "Hero". By Mariah Carey. Acapella?'

'Yep,' I said.

Her concern should have been an indication of how the performance would play out. But rose-coloured-glasses Deni was keen to have their American high school musical moment.

I stood there on stage for approximately three minutes and sang 'Hero' by Mariah Carey. Without missing a beat. The thing about singing acapella, however, is that you don't have any background music to drown out the hurls of abuse being thrown your way. Between each verse and consistently throughout I heard cries of 'faggot' and 'poof'. I also heard the occasional senior girl standing up and turning around to yell, 'Leave him alone!' I knew it was a disaster, but I refused to stop singing, if you could call it that, until I finished the final, very high, very long, awkward note.

Was I bullied every single day for the rest of my high school experience? You better fucking believe I was. Did I ever once show the bullies that their bullying got to me? Absolutely not. Did I cry myself to sleep and write about my own self-loathing in my diary every single night for two years straight? Yes. I did. I also never sang at a talent quest again. The bullying was just not worth the experience.

I did, however, find solace in dance.

One blessing of attending Geelong High School was that it had an exceptional performing arts centre and a program that facilitated a safe space for all humans who had no interest in playing sports. From school productions to dance concerts, our small but mighty performing arts hub was the home I yearned for throughout much of my high school existence. I might not have been one of the cool kids, but I didn't care. In those halls I fell in love with choreography and rhythm and self-expression and collaboration and event planning, costume design and camaraderie.

That's the thing about nonconformity: every so often you are blessed to find another group of nonconforming humans you get to call chosen family. I rarely see the girls from my dance class these days, or my incredible dance teachers, but you can be sure that when I do there is nothing but a nostalgic reminder of that love. The nostalgic reminders of us all falling in love with *Moulin Rouge*, of obsessing over Julia Stiles' performance in the movie *Save the Last Dance*. The afternoons spent rehearsing and perfecting every last cannon and kickball change so that come the night of our concerts, we gave our guests a SHOW.

On that dance stage, my flamboyance was celebrated. My femininity was applauded and my uniqueness commended. I was one of only two masc-presenting humans who took dance class from Year 9 through to Year 12 and you could feel the excitement in the air whenever one of us was on stage. The audience ate it up. In the schoolyard we barely spoke to one another, but in that dance hall there was an unspoken shared experience between us. In those moments we were proud of our nonconformity, and looking back now, I'm just as proud.

Not all humans find spaces to revel in their nonconforming spirit. So many compromise their authentic selves in order to be liked by their peers and win the affection of the ones they love. But shouldn't authenticity provide the beginning and flow of any healthy relationship? As someone who has ducked and weaved their way around, walking that fine line between concealing who I truly am and letting my freak flag fly, I promise you the latter is far more rewarding.

When I spoke to Elise about the long-term toll that the pressure to conform can take on us all, she said: 'When we talk about conformity, we're essentially discussing authentic expression. When our authentic expression is not approved, we resort to building masks and therefore defences to conceal it. The more disapproval your expression receives, the more likely you are to overdo the masks. Within this we also see a lot of internalised phobias and identity unrest start to form. As a result, the more performative we are as humans, the more likely we are to create a life for ourselves that will implode. It implodes as it's not aligned to your core self.'

Talk about an A-HA moment!

Queer people often have seasons of life like the cycle Elise described to me. You typically spend most of your adolescence absolutely hating your Queerness. You despise it. You reject it. You suppress it. You put one mask over the other mask and the one underneath that, and to be honest sometimes the masks just never come off. If you do choose to come out and live your authentic expression, you are then welcomed with the plethora of choice in a new world – only to find that within this world exist so many subcultures, with their own rules and groupthink. And it's up to you whether you lean into them or not. Will you be a sub or a dom? A top or a bottom? A twink or a bear?

Subcultures likely exist in your backyard too. You might even find them somewhere as mundane as the school drop-off.

You know the mum. The Cool Mum. She drops her kids off at school in the morning and she's effortlessly stylish. Her look is P.E Nation activewear if she lives in Sydney and Jaggad activewear if she lives in Melbourne. She's wearing oversized Porsche Carrera aviator sunglasses. She drives a Rangey but she doesn't brag about it, ya know? She has that no-make-up-make-up look and you can't begin to fathom how she 'bounced back' so quickly. Except that you know exactly how, because you follow her on Instagram and you know she does reformer Pilates. She drinks soy lattes and green juices, but also loves a cheeky cigarette and a glass of rosé on a Friday afternoon. Her hair is shiny. Her life is good.

Can we talk about the inner city #millennial for a hot minute? He lives in Brunswick, works in graphic design and cycles to work most days. He hates his job and will tell anyone who listens but is also really 'bloody proud' of the brand identity he just finished for this niche gin distillery. He drinks oat milk, craft beer and gin and tonics with a cucumber if he's feeling fancy. He wears Le Labo Santal and carries a Fjällräven Kånken backpack in navy, because his 'cooler' man crush at work has one in black. He goes to the pub with his colleagues every Friday night and is definitely withdrawing $350 at the ATM on his way. He listens to the *Inspired Unemployed* podcast. He wears a freshly pressed vintage shirt to the bar on a Saturday night with some Carhartt trousers and a pair of Docs, and he's smiling at the girl he's just been introduced to. He uses a thirty-dollar shampoo, so his hair is shiny. His life is good.

Then there's the subculture of the #blessed girls. They all went to high school together and played on the same netball team. Their salt-of-the-earth boyfriends proposed to them over the summer period and now your newsfeed is filled with their celebrations for 'wedding SZN'. They wear Zimmermann. They drink Aperol spritzes. They listen to Zara and Michelle on their early morning walks. Their coffees are made with almond milk and they get HelloFresh delivered, because it's honestly so convenient and also they got a discount code from their favourite influencer. Their Instagram stories are consumed by gratitude because they're #blessed. Their hair is shiny. Their lives are good.

I could go on listing these subcultures all day. Truly.

Full disclosure: I know many humans who belong to these subcultures and I LOVE THAT FOR THEM. (In fact, I myself resonate with many of these personality traits. I am and will always be a basic bitch from the suburbs at heart. Trust.) This was not a diss track. ILYSM. I would also like to state, for the record, that there is not one iota of shame in moments of conformity. I have conformed in more ways over the years than I can count, from the haircuts I got to try and fit in, to the fake Louis Vuitton bag that I begged my mum to get me in Bali. It's all about being self-aware in these moments on why and how you're conforming. Okay: now take a deep breath and meet me below when you're ready.

Conformity is everywhere. Uniforms – those pesky masks we put on until we implode – are everywhere.

So where are you among all of this?

We've come to the portion of this chapter where it's time for you to go inwards. Because if I've learned anything in rebelling against the norm, it's that in authentic expression comes true liberation. The big, overarching question we're going to ask ourselves is: *In what ways has my identity today been shaped by experiences of conformity?*

If you need a hand getting started, may I suggest that we do a little exercise together. Take this book along with you (or note down to do the exercise after you've finished this chapter).

 Over to you, darling

Step 1

Walk over to your wardrobe. Open it, look inside. Does the clothing hanging in front of you look like you? Like REALLY look like you? Or is what you see a visual representation of a subculture you've subscribed to? Do the clothes you own spark joy in your soul, or have they been purchased out of an internal desire to 'fit in'? Have you ever got dressed and then undressed out of fear of what others might think? Have you ever bought overpriced activewear just because an influencer on Instagram made you feel like you'd be cooler if you did?

Step 2

Take a look at your surroundings. Your bedroom, perhaps your apartment, home, shared living space. Are you reflected within it? Similar to your wardrobe, do you see elements of your authentic identity in your everyday environment?

Step 3

This one is a little more internal. Is the way you are currently earning a living something of your choosing? Or if you're studying, does your course or degree align with your own personal interests? Does your job or career path authentically reflect who you are inside? Have you chosen that degree or career path because society told you that you should?

Step 4

Let's go a bit deeper. Take yourself to a mirror and look at the vessel that carries your spirit. Is it an authentic reflection of how you feel inside or have you tailored it to fit into a mould that society has shaped for you? Is the way you present outwardly reflecting who you are internally?

Take your time with all of this. Get specific. After working through each reflection, write down the ways in which conformity has impacted your identity and likely the course of your life. It's only once you've separated what is authentic from what is inauthentic that you can start to course-correct back to following YOUR path, choreographing your own dance routine, living life on your own terms.

You might notice that your answers to the questions above overlap with some of the work we did in chapters 1 and 2. So often our all-important influences like family, culture and childhood trauma inform the messages we receive: *You must be accepted. You must fit in. You must not stand out. You must follow the same path as your parents or, at the very least, your best friend Becky.*

What I'm encouraging here is that you equip yourself with the right tools so when the internal alarm Elise spoke about goes off – when we implode because we realise the life that we're living doesn't align with our core self – you will have the agency and sense of self to give it the big finger and say, 'FUCK YOU VERY MUCH. I will do as I choose. I will honour my authentic identity. I will honour my inner child and that, frankly, is no one's business but mine.'

Does it feel as good for you to read as it does for me? I fucking hope so.

Now I want us to flip the script and work on some answers, because remember, I'm a solutions kinda human.

Think ahead to the type of life you could be living if you chose to dance to the beat of your own drum and align your life to the desires of your authentic self. Really visualise yourself in this position: where you live, what you're doing for work, the humans you're surrounding yourself with, how they treat you and how you treat them. Your hobbies and interests. Your sense of self and your lifestyle.

Now that you've spent a bit of time visualising this new and improved life, answer each of the following questions:

- In what ways will nonconformity impact my identity?
- What is, at its core, my own version of authentic expression?
- In what ways can I enhance and celebrate my authentic expression?
- What are some things I can actively do to get closer to it?
- How will the above make me feel?

If you want to get really excited and let your mind drift to the possibilities of your authentic expression, I'd love you to join me in a visualisation exercise. This is a perfect way to dip your toes into a practice that me and so many others swear by.

 Over to you, darling

When it comes to attracting the life you want, one of the most crucial elements is belief. Listen to any interview of someone society deems successful, let's say Lady Gaga, and you'll hear a recurring theme. That against all the odds they believed in themselves. Intuitively. Unconditionally. Spiritually. Lady Gaga could feel she was going to be an Oscar winner long before she held that gold man in her hands.

Such is the power of self-belief and, as a necessary means of executing this self-belief, the power of visualisation.

Whether we realise it or not, we 'visualise' hypotheticals for ourselves every single day, and have done so since childhood. The key is to visualise with intention; that's when shit gets real.

I've been surrounded by vision boards ever since I was a teenager; even though I didn't call them that back then, I was always aware of the power they yield. There's something incredibly fulfilling about looking at a visual cue every day to remind you of your intentions, your goals and dreams, whether it's a holiday you want to go on, a family you wish to create, a life change you want to call in or a car you want to buy.

Today you're going to start with a vision board that reflects your authentic expression, in spite of conformist pressures. We'll use the following questions as cues. When there is no uniform to wear, and you realise you don't need to live according to societal standards and stereotypes, who are you?

Step 1

Write down five keywords that describe who you are. These should have nothing to do with how you physically look. I want you to think about your insides. Use adjectives. Get creative.

Step 2

Think about how these keywords look like both in your mind and in the world. Are there colours, moods, films, music, cities, art, shapes and/or silhouettes that represent your key spirit? Here's an example:

One of my keywords is BOLD. When I think of the word bold, I think of the colour red, I think animal print, I think sharp shoulders and high stilettos. I think of resilient trailblazers who stand firm in their identity. I think of whisky on the rocks, of 'Diva' by Beyoncé and New York City. See how the images of a word start to flow?

Step 3

Now that you have some references that inform who you are, I want you to start looking for images that reflect that. Get your Pinterest game on, tear up Google Images or go old school and pull out magazine images that speak to your soul. They can vary from a flower to a cityscape, to a colour palette, to a style icon, to a film poster, quote or song lyric. This is the fun part where you can get lost in your imagination. Play some music, pour yourself a drink and relish in this moment. You're building your own life, one image at a time.

Step 4

Ideally you would save these images, print them out and group them together to stick up somewhere that's visible to you. (I know that household printers are a rarity these days, so maybe you make a trip out for this exercise. Take them to your local Officeworks to print off, or use the printer at work, uni, school, etc.) If you don't do it the old-school way, perhaps make a Pinterest board or create a digital collage that you can then use as your lockscreen wallpaper on your phone. However, I have found that IRL vision boards are most effective. It's seeing the visual on a wall that works best for me!

Step 5

Once you have your collection of images somewhere you can see them, I want you to feel them. I want you to soak in what they mean to you, close your eyes and visualise the way they manifest in your expression and in your life.

If your wall is full of colour and you have nothing but black in your wardrobe, it's time to reconnect with who you truly are.

This visual example of your spirit will help you take a step back and evaluate your life more broadly. Is your external life reflecting who you are internally, at your core? If the answer is no, that's a call for change – remembering that change needn't happen all at once. Sometimes all it takes is the perfect red lipstick to set you on the right path.

Good luck and have fun! If you feel comfortable sharing your vision boards with me (and the internet), chuck them up in your Insta stories and tag @stylebydeni, because I would love to see them.

Pro tip: It's entirely up to you whether or not you choose to share your vision board with anyone other than yourself. But the act of sharing it does show confidence and conviction. This vision board should be something that you're proud to share, even if it's with just one person in your life, because essentially you're sharing yourself with the world – and angel, YOU are something to be so very proud of!

I reckon it's about time for a dance break.

Our song to start is very dear to me. If you haven't seen the film *The Greatest Showman* (2017), please add it to your watch list. It's a story of identity told so beautifully it took my breath away. The theme song is next level, and we're going to listen to it shortly, but can I also suggest you find the YouTube version in which Keala Settle sings it for the first time in rehearsal; in that moment, Hugh Jackman (who plays P. T. Barnum) looks up from the table behind her with tear-filled eyes. It never fails to make me ugly-cry, in the best possible way. Have tissues at the ready.

See you in four minutes fifty.

🎠 **Dance break** 🎠

'This Is Me' – Keala Settle, from *The Greatest Showman*
Once you've listened to this song, pause for a moment and then come back here.

Are you a blubbering mess? Me too, darling. The lyrics are about standing firm in your skin, in precisely who you are, flaws and all, masks thrown to the ground, for the world to see. It takes my breath away every single time.

Now make your way to the next track. This is a slightly more groove-along anthem of liberation: I've been obsessed with it since I was a teenager hearing it for the first time. Press Play on:

'Free' – Ultra Naté

Did you need that vibe shift as much as I did? I thought so.

As we close this chapter, having started all of these big, big reflections on who we are and where we've come from, can I just say, I'm really bloody proud of you. Doing the work is hard. Some people never do it. But you are here doing this work, so please give yourself a moment to be present and to be proud of yourself.

The main stage

I was asked to give a speech at my high school by a woman who manages relationships around leadership in former Geelong High School alumni. (Come to think of it, it sounds very American high school movie.) At this point, I'd moved back home with my parents after leaving *Cosmopolitan* magazine. That had been a dream job of mine that I'd worked towards for years, and I'd been immensely proud of my work there, but sadly the magazine had announced its closure and our whole team was made redundant.

Geelong is the type of place where if you achieve any level of success outside of it, and you return to the town, you're basically treated like Kim Kardashian – and I say that with deep, deep gratitude.

The school was looking for an 'inspiring former student' to present at their annual R U OK? Day assembly. For those unfamiliar, R U OK? Day is an annual event that zooms in on mental health and encourages us all to check in with the ones around us and to hold space for these conversations. In that moment I had a chance to capture the attention of a thousand high school students who were getting ready to go into the world and (hopefully) make it better. I needed to make an impact.

When the day came around my mum asked me what I might wear. I told her I was going to wear what I always wished I could have worn to school all those years ago. I put on a boxy crisp navy short-sleeve shirt. I tucked my shirt into a pleated, navy kilt, made from a wool-crepe so it had just enough structure but also the right amount of flow to swish its way around my body. I teamed the look with a pair of black, ten-centimetre-heel ankle boots. The school may have kept me in those trousers for more than a decade, but I would return in a motherfucking kilt. OKURR.

As I made my way up the stairs, nervous as all hell, I was welcomed with cheers and applause and comments like 'YASS KWEEN, GET IT'. My, how far we've come.

The following is a much-abridged version of the speech I gave that day:

FAGGOT. POOFTER. HOMO. These are just some of the names I was called at this school. On this very stage, in fact. My name, however, is Deni Todorović. I am gay, and I'm a former student of your school.

Words, and the way we use them, can hold so much power. I was bullied every single day from Year 7 to halfway through Year 11; I used to keep a journal, and I remember on one specific day counting six separate occasions that I had been on the receiving end of bullying. This had happened throughout primary school too.

I vividly remember sitting in this hall before an assembly when three girls in my year level pestered me with questions like, 'Are you that gay boy? Do you have a boyfriend? Have you ever even kissed a girl?' I said no to these questions, the ones that scared me most. I sat back in my seat, fighting back tears. No was my answer and I was sticking to it – because I wasn't going to become the words they used to describe me.

I was lucky enough to have the support of a handful of friends and cousins who also went to this school, and there were some incredible teachers who became my real saviours in those years, giving me an identity outside of this bullying. They nurtured my creative talent, writing roles for me in school productions, encouraging my love of dance, and introducing me to the joyous escape that is reading a good book. I'm forever grateful to these teachers who helped me bloom into the person who stands before you today.

Nonetheless, those words continued: Faggot. Poofter. Homo. I developed a thick skin, but this also meant that I repressed the feeling deep down that I wasn't normal.

What is the power of words like those? Let me share some statistics with you. In Australia, as of 2018, LGBTQIA+ young people are five times more likely to attempt suicide than their straight counterparts. In the transgender community, that figure jumps to eleven times more likely. Thirty-three percent of LGBTQIA+ youth have self-harmed, and a staggering 53 percent of trans youth. LGBTQIA+ Australians are more likely to become involved with substance abuse and to experience homelessness.

These are not just words. Each time you make the choice to call your classmate a dyke or a faggot, you push them further away, and you have no idea of the long-term consequences for their self-esteem, their self-worth, their mental health, their life.

Here's the thing: I didn't want to be defined by these labels, or to become these statistics. So I shook the hate off and went on my own journey of self-discovery. I came out, something my thirteen-year-old self would've never thought possible. The world didn't come crumbling down around me. I've gone on to make a career and a livelihood out of those creative talents that my teachers nurtured so carefully in me. I can't even imagine what thirteen-year-old Deni would think of me wearing heels in front of you all, in their old school hall.

The reality is that high school means very little in the grand scheme of life. It doesn't matter if you were the most popular girl at school, the hottest jock on the football field, the tallest, the wealthiest, the poorest, the geek, the immigrant. All these labels society forces on you mean nothing, ultimately. Because pretty soon you'll find yourself in the big, wide world and no one will care. What people will care about are your values: the way you treat other people and the way you make them feel. People will always remember how you made them feel.

And this is where tolerance comes in. You may not understand why your best mate likes dudes, or why your best girlfriend is into chicks. You may not understand why your friend in Year 7 intuitively knows that he has been assigned a gender he now doesn't identify with, and that by Year 9 he feels it's time to start his transition. You might not understand why another mate goes to the mosque on Sundays. Or why your best friends has two dads, or two mums, or just one parent. You may never understand why the girl on your netball team can't afford the latest pair of Nike sneakers, because her dad's an alcoholic and her mum is working her ass off to support their family. You might not understand why someone is different to you, and that's okay – it's not your lived experience. But what you must always strive for is to exercise tolerance and, even better than that, acceptance of difference. Compassion. Support.

The event organiser later told me that in all the years they'd had guest speakers in this hall, they'd never heard it more quiet or seen the students more engaged. This meant a tremendous amount to me because, on that day, I felt like I was having an out-of-body experience.

There I was, standing on the same stage that I had been ridiculed on. Yet here I was, years later, confident in my own skin, celebrated for my authentic expression, passing on the baton for the students to do the same.

Affirmation

I reject what society asks me to be and I will revel in who
I truly am.

I am love.
I move with love.

I love you.
The real you.

4.

Let's talk about sex

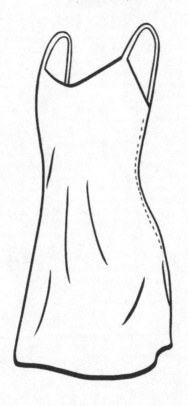

S ex and sexuality have the power to mould the very essence of the soul, to shape our deepest desires alongside our darkest of insecurities. Our relationships with sex and sexuality involve enormous emotional investment. They can become great tools of power or debilitating shackles of the shame so often attached to them. Coming out of said shame, for so many, can be a lifelong process.

For some, sexual shame never completely leaves us. It creeps up during moments of both private and relational intimacy, in ways we might least expect. What we can do to relieve that shame is to unpack, 'come out', heal and glide through it, rather than against it.

Our roadmap to living authentically stops in at this complex, thorny and vulnerable subject area because our sexuality is informed by those big, important influences we've been looking at so far, like family and culture and institutional conformity. Some of these influences are more visible and easier to understand than others.

In the previous chapter we learnt to separate our authentic self from conformist pressures, and here we'll continue that journey. Our sexuality is shaped by our desire to be accepted by others and to meet some kind of manufactured standard for what is 'normal'. It's the reason so many teenagers vow to lose their virginity at the same time. Why so many of us felt inadequate when we remained the only human standing at graduation never having kissed another pair of lips.

We compare ourselves at every given turn, measuring our trajectories of sexual desire and experience against those around us and those who came before us. Throughout my adolescence I constantly heard that my dad was a 'ladies' man', so imagine my feelings of inadequacy when I became the total opposite: someone who was considered 'frigid', then a 'faggot', the last person in my friendship group to so much as even touch another human sexually.

Sexuality – regardless of your gender identity, which genders you're attracted to and your level of sexual libido – has likely informed your identity more than you even realise. Or maybe you do realise, and you know that those early pressures to look, to want and to behave a certain way have been holding you back from your own pleasures and liberty as an adult.

Let's look into that, shall we?

This is going to be a deep chapter and may potentially be triggering. So just a warning up-front that this section will cover topics of sexual abuse and trauma. I will leave you with some resources of support at the end. Remember that this book is a safe space and our conversation, while shared, is also private. Right now, it's just you and me, along with a few curated thoughts, critical analysis, wisdom (hopefully) and intentional healing (definitely).

So, my darling, go fix yourself a cuppa and pour yourself something soothing, then let's get stuck right in.

We're going to start with a story, as we always do. I'm going to take you back once again to my childhood. I told you earlier in this book that I became aware of my own, let's call it 'sexiness', from a very young age. I chalk up my early awareness of sexuality to my obsession with sex-positive trailblazers in the music industry like Janet Jackson and Madonna. I was always drawn to music with sexual subtext, and while I'm sure I didn't fully grasp the meaning of the lyrics I danced along to, I will always remember how empowered such songs made me feel, much to the embarrassment of my mama. For example, I vividly remember being told off by her for loudly singing 'Let's Talk About Sex' by Salt-N-Pepa at a family function.

Another memory stands out to me. As I've said, my feminine nature as a child often found expression in the articles of clothing I felt drawn to. I noticed that boys were given cotton pyjamas and boxer shorts to sleep in, while girls got to wear beautiful silk nightgowns and slip dresses. The female characters in *Days of Our Lives* always wore the most stunning silk and satin sleepwear, and the sensuality they represented was alluring to me. I used to hate my cotton pyjamas, covered in trucks and various other 'boy-appropriate' prints.

One afternoon, when I was around seven or eight years old, Mum and Dad left me and my brother at home while they took a trip to Harvey Norman. My brother was outside playing with our dog and before he could even shut the sliding door, I made a beeline for my mother's bedside table and opened each drawer, until I found what I was looking for. I pulled it towards me, a sea of satin and silk, its texture picking up the sunlight.

My mum's slip dress was coloured somewhere between navy and midnight blue. I always loved how glamorous it made her look, just like the dresses women wore on the cover of the Mills & Boon novels I'd found in a box when we'd moved house a year earlier. I wanted to feel as sensual as those women looked, so at that moment I took off my school polo shirt, making sure to leave my trackpants on. I poured the slip dress over my arms, one by one, and felt the satin hit my bare chest. I spun around the room and made my way towards a mirror. I admired my reflection. I felt alive. I felt sexy. I felt liberated.

… and then, I felt ashamed.

I took the slip off after less than a minute and put it back in the drawer. I then ran to my bedroom to cry into my pillow.

Why did I do that? What was I thinking? Why, oh why, did it feel so damn good?

The answers to my questions are very simple now, but it wasn't always so clear to me.

It's widely acknowledged how deeply formative our earliest years of life can be in relation to our sexual identity. In order for you and me to be sexually untroubled adults requires that, way back, others will have left us feeling acceptable to ourselves, enjoying a sense that our bodies and their functions were natural things; that it was neither 'naughty' nor 'sinful' to express curiosity about our bodily pleasures.

Sexual desire is one of the most personal and vulnerable emotions we will ever express, and for that reason, those very desires can also lead to great shame and ridicule. It's been said many times that if you want to hurt someone fast, shame them about their sexuality, and they'll seldom have the confidence to challenge you again. I know this to be true, I've got the receipts to prove it. Something tells me you may too.

Can you pinpoint the moment you first became aware of sex? For me it was very much via film and television. Disney was responsible for planting the idea that for every damsel in distress came a hunky man from the village to save her, with brute physique and perfectly coiffed hair and a life-saving kiss to boot. It was Hollywood that introduced me to sex scenes, always skipped through by my parents, who were quick to change the channel or hit that fast-forward button when we watched movies or shows as a family.

Despite this, my family was never 'prudish' when it came to the topic of sex education. I was seven years old when Dad sat me and my brother down to give us 'the talk'. One day after picking us up from school, he gave us a very adult breakdown of what sex was, where babies came from and what we might expect as our bodies changed and we made the transition into puberty. He used 'grown-up' terminology and even drew diagrams. He wanted us to have a clear understanding of sex rather than allow my brother and me to hear incorrect versions in the playground.

That conversation opened up the floodgates and shortly thereafter he would explain to us what puberty would entail. On our car rides home from school, we'd discuss pubic hair, erections, porn, masturbation and wet dreams. By this stage I was a little bit older, closer to ten or eleven. I remember that my first wet dream was, to my dad's mind, a moment as formative as a young human menstruating for the first time. My dad explained to us what would happen and advised that when we woke up the morning after, we might have 'sticky jocks', but not to fear as that was just semen. He told us to just take our sticky jocks and put them in the laundry basket so that Mum wouldn't have to. Bless his soul. He would ask me on occasion if it had 'happened yet'. When I told him it hadn't, he would reassure me, 'It's nothing to be embarrassed about, Deni, it's natural.' In retrospect I'm really glad he added that declaration.

Except that it did happen, and I was embarrassed.

I'll never forget my first wet dream. Afterwards I felt waves of shame spiral through my mind and body. Pleasure combined with shame would go on to become a toxic combination that followed me into my adult life.

The following morning, as promised, my jocks were in fact 'sticky', and they served as a reminder of the shame I felt the night before. Every time after, whenever I would put my 'sticky jocks' in the laundry basket, I would feel those pangs of shame. When my dad next asked me if it had happened yet, I couldn't bear to tell him, because my wet dreams involved men. He never asked me again, and I was grateful he respected that boundary.

I don't particularly recall sex education at school being adequate to equip a bunch of teenagers with a nuanced understanding of the journey we were all about to embark on. I do remember that my senior coordinator, along with my health teacher, asked if I would be more comfortable taking sex ed with my female classmates rather than with the boys. Perhaps they sensed then what I know now. I accepted that offer with much enthusiasm and gratitude. I couldn't think of anything worse than being in a classroom with my immature male counterparts, who would no doubt giggle at the mere mention of the word 'erection' and likely taunt me about the discussions of dicks and sex.

So I sat in that classroom with my AFAB students, learning about periods, contraception and female anatomy. In retrospect perhaps I should have sat in with 'the boys' and learnt more about my own body, but I felt comfortable and safe in a classroom filled with feminine energy.

The whole process was a very straight, very binary one. Homosexuality and sexual orientation weren't part of the syllabus, nor was gender identity. How humans were supposed to be taught such complex subject matter in a short period of time perplexed me. It seemed like a checkbox our teachers were forced to tick, and it was nothing as progressive as I saw recently play out in the Netflix series *Sex Education*. (If you haven't already seen it, put it at the top of your must-watch list.)

The halls and yards of my high school were a hotbed of sexual trauma. Slut-shaming was rife. There was a girl in our year who told her friend she enjoyed masturbating. She shared this with someone she thought she could trust, in confidence. By lunchtime word had spread and by the next day, derogatory nicknames were formed. In home room, one group of boys turned around to ask this girl if she 'fingers herself' and how often. Her response was nothing short of iconic: 'Yeah, I do it every day and it feels fucking great, so get fucked.' When the boys' shocked faces turned to giggles, I heard them call her a slut under their breath; when she finished giving them the finger, our eyes met. For a moment, I saw shame behind her 'fuck you' bravado. Sadness, even. I gave her a look of support.

+✦+

Shortly after those sticky dreams began, I discovered what my body could do if I touched it just enough. I found out that thrusting against pillows and mattresses could build up to release, and later I realised that the shortcut was quite literally in the palm of my hands. I found out via a movie. A young man in his twenties returns from a date after the girl he went out with rejected his offer to come home with him. So he proceeds to rush home to go to the bathroom and pulls out a *Playboy* magazine. That wasn't the only thing he was pulling, let me tell you. (Did I just make a dad joke? Forgive me.)

When I tell you I RAN to the toilet, shut the door behind me and put this method to test so fast – I mean it. Suffice to say, I went to the toilet a lot that summer. But afterwards, as I caught my breath post-orgasm, the feelings of awe at what my body could do, and just how much pleasure that release gave me, was always followed with an overwhelming sense of guilt.

When my dad had first explained masturbation to my brother and me, he prefaced it by explaining that the Bible, and therefore God, considers masturbation to be sinful. I should add that he reminded us God understands we are all imperfect humans with hormones, and so we shouldn't feel bad about masturbating. He did say that we shouldn't do it too often. I'm not sure what was considered too often, but I can assure you when teenagers discover masturbation they're doing it a whole lot.

The fact is that the Bible is both vague and direct when it comes to what it deems to be sinful, and while you won't find a scripture that says 'Don't jerk off in the toilets', if you read between the lines you will find many that speak to it. From scriptures declaring you must do everything in the glory of God, to a scripture that loosely touches on a man 'spilling his seed' on the ground. In Chapter 38 of The Book of Genesis, Onan was accused of masturbation and, for this supposed transgression, was struck dead by God. In our church there was a message shared that 'if you wouldn't do it in front of Jesus, it's probably wrong'. Because Jesus would have no issues with a couple 'making love', but as for 'fucking' and 'self-pleasure' – apparently not so much, hun.

The messages around masturbation can be even more confusing if you're a woman, or if you're Queer. In an article titled 'Masturbation Shame Is Deeply Ingrained in Us, but We Can Undo It' published on *Refinery 29*, sex coach Georgia Grace says the following on the topic: 'sexual scripts teach that masturbation is something young boys can joke about, compare stories and even bond over – they are taught masturbation is an impulse and something very normal. Though, for girls, women and LGBTQIA+ young people, they are taught that the very thought of them touching their body for pleasure is shameful, disgusting and wrong.'

Grace continues, 'Many people experience sexual shame as a result of limited education, misleading information, no access to sex-positive spaces or opportunities to inquire, religious teachings that condemn sex beyond procreation, and culture of taboo around sex, bodies and relationships. It's setting people up for a lifetime of confusion and not so great sexual experiences.'

Every time I touched myself while thinking about Aaron, the cute new boy in my Year 9 class, or the naked torso that appeared on the packaging of my new Bonds trunks, I felt sinful, disgusting and ashamed. Afterwards I'd wash and wash and wash my hands repeatedly. I would make promises to God that I would never masturbate again, counting the days between each time. When I would inevitably 'relapse', the shame spiral would start all over again. This pattern continued well into my late teens and, if I'm honest, it's a feeling that, on a very minor scale, I don't think will ever leave me.

Think for a moment just how many 'pro-pleasure' campaigns you see on your socials. In the past couple of years, influencers have filled the newsfeeds of women and Queer people to share with us their latest lifestyle recommendations, only in place of lip gloss they're now holding dildos and vibrators and love eggs and lube and frankly, WE LOVE TO SEE IT. You can't help but wonder why there's a need to promote something so heavily that should be a natural form of pleasure. No one should have to sell you pleasure, it should be inherent. A universal truth that we rightfully deserve. Yet here we are, one by one, trying to break down the chains of sexual oppression we've been wrapped in for most of our adolescence, in many cases since our childhood.

Don't even get me started on pornography. Do you remember your first encounter with porn? Mine was during the summer holidays when I was about eleven. My uncle had a stash of nude magazines I stumbled upon by accident. This was very pre-internet times and it wouldn't be for another seven years that I discovered free gay porn online. And when I did, it was a revelation of sorts: as a gay person, when mainstream media offers you nothing more than a tokenistic man-on-man kiss in a film or two, you have little to no option but to search for your sexual self on the worldwide often-dark web.

Porn can be a source of liberation while also being incredibly damaging in the way it distorts our overall perception of sex. I myself have made excuses for certain types of behaviour in the bedroom based off my earliest interactions with porn. I've even behaved in certain ways sexually because of it. Over the years, porn has made me hate my body, agonise over the lack of a perfectly chiselled sixpack, not to mention the size of my penis, because it could always be bigger, couldn't it? The anxiety of it all. And then, when you look deeper at the way porn affects cis women and trans folks, and particularly the ways that cis men approach sex with women, it takes little to no effort to connect the dots between porn and accepting poor behaviour.

We live in a 'confessional' society, a concept that perhaps ironically stems from the Catholic Church. Every week, in places of worship around the world, humans make their way into a private booth to confess their sins to 'men of god' and pray for forgiveness. They do so because anxiety shared is anxiety halved. Trauma shared is trauma halved. 'Sin' shared is – well, you get the picture. You cannot ask for forgiveness if you do not first confess what it is you are seeking forgiveness for. Only that pleasure is not a sin, sexual awakening is not sinful and yet anyone that's grown up in a faith-based environment will tell you that both feelings are almost always in adolescence riddled with guilt and shame. Sometimes never to leave us.

This concept of confession now exists beyond the Catholic Church. Look no further than TikTok or Instagram or wherever it is you stream your podcasts and you will find a plethora of 'confessions' shared with the world, one 'hot take' after another 'let's unpack this' after another 'can we normalise ...' Trauma is shared so frequently on social media in the hope of finding community, a group of humans that understand; of finding space, craving to be held.

Coming out in and of itself is much like confessing. Coming out asks us to bare our soul and speak our identities – our deepest and most vulnerable sense of who we are – aloud. It asks us to step into our own truth. It's only in confessing who we are that we begin to construct our authentic identity anew.

I've bared all of my awkward adolescent sexual experiences with you, my dear reader, to inspire you to connect the dots about your own experiences with sexual shame and guilt, and how they might have shaped your own desires as an adult, your own sex lives and behaviours, and your own capacity for sexual pleasure and liberation.

I should add the caveat that this was my lived experience and I have a penis, for Christ's sake! I'm fully cognisant of my 'penis privilege' entering into this discussion. Misogyny goes hand in hand with sexual oppression and repression; the sexualisation of women from girlhood and their objectification in popular culture has real-world implications for women's bodily autonomy and safety.

I grew up in an era where a particular brand of misogyny reigned supreme, where Paris Hilton and Kim Kardashian became laughing-stocks because of men who leaked private sex tapes. Where paparazzi culture ridiculed Britney Spears and Lindsay Lohan for not wearing underwear. In a time where it took a show like *Sex and the City* to show a kind of modern woman gaining a degree of agency over her own sexuality, albeit while likely whispering judgement to anyone who even remotely identified as a 'Samantha'.

I grew up in a pre-MeToo world, where I heard, more than I'd like to recall, sentences like, 'Well, she was asking for it. What was she wearing?' In a time when, after allegations of abuse of a woman by a man, the blame – the sexual shame and guilt – was shifted onto her to become, against her will, her responsibility; her lifelong burden to bear.

The scent of toxic masculinity permeates so many areas of our life, a scent as strong as the Lynx Java your teenage classmates wore. We bear witness to the far-reaching impacts of toxic masculinity on the streets of our cities, in the halls of our schools, in the offices of our workplaces and in the walls of our own parliament.

So how, oh-fucking-how, does one even begin to unpack and heal through sexual shame in all its horrific manifestations?

Well. I think first we need some deep breaths. Will you breathe with me? Let's take three, deep, breaths. In and out. Ready?

One.

Two.

Three.

Thank you, I needed that. I do that when things feel a little heavy.

Looking at your own discomfort around sex, sexuality and shame is the first step to healing and liberation. One can't both hate themselves, their body and their sexual identity and have a healthy relationship with their sex and sexuality. A fear of intimacy is typically a result of self-loathing. I didn't know that until a therapist told me, and then suddenly it became clear as day. So who made me hate myself? Because it sure as fuck wasn't me.

This is what we're going to unpack. Because we deserve to understand sex not as a place of shame, fear and trauma but rather as a tool to rediscover our own identities intimately: our likes and dislikes; the fun, experimental and empowering nature of sex. That's the kind of intimacy I've always craved and, I hazard a guess, that you've also felt at some point in your life.

It all starts with YOU.

First of all, ask yourself, what was your introduction to sex? Was it explained to you by a parent or guardian, or was it something you were left to learn out in the wild?

A recent survey I conducted on my socials suggests that over 80 percent of the people who responded were never sat down and given 'the talk' by their parents. Upon asking my mum the same question, she shared with me that she wasn't even informed of the fact she would one day have a period. The first time it happened she ran home from school, bleeding, to ask for her grandmother's help. 'But why wouldn't someone have told you beforehand?' I asked her. 'Because those things were not discussed,' she answered.

Now that you've answered that foundational question, I want you to think about the questions below. Sit with them for a while, and then you'll start to connect the dots.

 Over to you, darling

Sex

- Was sex framed to you in a positive light?
- Was it framed to you alongside words like 'naughty' and 'cheeky'?
- Was it framed to you as an equal-opportunity part of life, or was it enforced with a side of misogyny, religion, homophobia and shame?

- For the vulva owners reading, did the emphasis on the reproductive nature of your sexuality hold precedence over your own pleasure and body autonomy?

Love

- Were love and affection shown to you as a child in a way that is healthy or toxic?
- Did your parents tell you they loved you?
- How often did you hear it growing up?
- How often do they tell you now?
- Have your siblings or close relatives ever made negative comments about your sex and sexuality?

Body image

- Did anyone ever teach you to love and respect your body?
- Were you ever taught to love yourself? To speak highly of your body?
- Has your body been the topic of dinner-table conversation or idle gossip between your relatives?
- Were you bullied about your body at school, in the hallway, in the locker room, on the schoolyard?
- Have you been treated differently because of your body?

Pleasure

- Did anyone ever teach you to honour and respect the pleasure you so rightfully deserve?
- Was masturbation something you were taught to enjoy and explore with curiosity? Or was that riddled with shame too?
- Have you ever been slut-shamed? Wolf-whistled at – or worse?

Identity

- Have you been made to feel unsafe because of your sexuality and/or gender identity?
- Have you ever heard your appearance being talked about in a negative light?
- Have you been judged or treated differently because of the gender assigned to you at birth or because of your sexuality?
- Are you afraid to even speak the truth of your sexual orientation out loud?

Consent

- Did you ever learn about consent in a formal or semi-formal setting? From anyone? By parents? Teachers? Family members? Friends?
- Was consent something you saw modelled in media growing up?

And here's where we'll really go deep on questions of consent and abuse — if you're not ready for that, that's completely understandable. Skip ahead to after this section, on page 107.

Have you, at any point in your life, had your own intimate sexual boundaries crossed, coerced or abused?

Let me go deeper for a moment, because you might be reading this thinking, *nah not really, I don't think so.* So I'll rephrase.

Have you ever at any point in your life been made to feel unsafe sexually?

And, on the other side of the coin: *Have you ever at any point in your life crossed the boundaries of another, coerced or abused someone sexually?*

This is a judgement-free space, and we are here to heal and grow together.

I want you to think about the above honestly and then start to connect the dots that make up your own sexual history. Unpack and compartmentalise, and develop a greater understanding of the shame that's likely linked to your sex and sexuality, and the way in which it is informing your relationships: the relationships with those around you and the most important relationship of all, the one with yourself.

Are you ready for a dance break? I think you've earned it, darling.

Dance break

If you have on any level been made to feel like a victim, either by an individual or an institution, you are a fighter. The first song I want to guide you towards is an absolute anthem for anyone who has survived trauma. I want you to sing this out loud; I want you to get up and stomp your feet and punch the air to your heart's content. Let's press Play on:

'Fighter' – Christina Aguilera

Now that we've acknowledged the fight, I invite us to look to healing and survival; it's time to make peace with the trauma and the way it has placed shackles on your identity.

The next song, written by a survivor of sexual abuse, never fails to deliver as therapy via song. I recommend turning the volume UP for:

'Praying' – Kesha

You back? Did that feel as cathartic for you as it did me?

I resonate so much with Kesha's sentiment in that song: I wholeheartedly believe that making peace with trauma, no matter how troubling a prospect that may seem at first, is, in my opinion, the key to healing. It doesn't mean you have to be nice, it doesn't mean you give that individual or the institution a get-out-of-jail-free card. Rather, it means you are giving yourself the freedom to no longer let that trauma restrain you.

Something that I want to highlight again here is that making peace with trauma is not a solo mission; as I've said, I began my healing journey well over ten years ago via three wonderful therapists. I would hope that these days, particularly in a post-pandemic world, therapy has lost much of its stigma and we've learnt how essential mental healthcare is. I began therapy via the mental health treatment plan, which allows you to claim up to twenty sessions with a mental health professional each year through Medicare. The plan is accessible, affordable and can be deeply helpful. I would say 90 percent of my friends have accessed therapy this way, and if the therapy game is new to you, you can too. Any GP in the country can put you on a mental health treatment plan.

When it came to finding the right therapist, my approach was by asking those around me. My first therapist was referred to me by a family member. My second was recommended by my gay friendship group in Sydney, and when I moved to Melbourne I asked some Queer friends if they could point me in the direction of an LGBTQIA+-friendly therapist; that was how I ended up at Thorne Harbour Health. Do some research into good therapists in your local area, and just know that, in general, finding a therapist that fits can be like finding the right hairdresser. It takes a level of commitment, and if someone doesn't feel like the right fit, you have the autonomy to reassess your options.

Some people may also find that more spiritual avenues are their preferred method for healing, or perhaps this complements therapy through more conventional means. Spirituality is certainly where my heart space sits now; whether it's reiki healing, EMDR therapy or holistic kinesiology, there is a big beautiful spiritual world out there. (More on all of this in Chapter 9.) However, I would suggest starting with the basics first: get yourself on a mental health treatment plan and get yourself into that therapist's chair.

That's how you'll begin your journey of putting the monsters to rest – sending them off, with peace and prayer, and making way for an internal peace of your own and a pride in who you are. Shame and all.

Freedom in a silk camisole

The email pinged through on a rather sombre day eight weeks into lockdown. I had only just come out as non-binary and I was still navigating the acceptance stage. Acceptance from myself. Acceptance from my family and acceptance from the greater world, which at this point consisted only by way of a digital community.

The email had been sent from a Melbourne-based lingerie brand. Their range consists mostly of silk camisole sets and robes, the kind my mum used to wear when I was a child and those glamorous women on *Days of Our Lives* used to sleep in. The brand had reached out to me after seeing me discuss the concept of de-gendering fashion on Instagram, asking if I would like them to send me some styles as a gift. They promised that there was no requirement for me to post, they just wanted me to enjoy their stunning pieces.

As I looked over their website a midnight-blue, silk, lace-trimmed camisole and short set caught my eye. I had never worn anything quite this feminine before, and if I'm honest, I was nervous as hell. My heart was beating out of my chest. As I sent my reply, thanking them kindly for their offer, I shot off my request for the silk set, my address and sizing, and walked away from my computer before I could change my mind.

What would people think? What would Mum and Dad think? Was this crossing a line?

I was instantly taken back to Little Deni in Mum's slip dress. Twirling around for ten seconds, then left stewing in shame.

It was time to rewrite my history and liberate myself through silk.

The package arrived much quicker than I had anticipated. As I opened the satchel, I saw tissue paper first, wrapped with a beautiful ribbon. Upon removing perfectly tied bows, I peeled back the paper to discover silk. The softest, most sensual silk, trimmed with the finest of laces, in the most seductive blue shade

I had ever seen. They'd even monogrammed it for me: on the left breast pocket, in white cursive font. *Deni.*

A silk camisole top of my own. With my fucking name on it. No stealing from Mum's closet necessary.

I held up the shorts, also trimmed with lace, and before I could think another thought, I made my way to my bedroom, shut that door and poured myself, finally, into silk of my own choosing. You know when silk hits your bare skin it feels first cold then warm? It's one of my favourite sensations, but a sensation that for the longest time had been associated with years of childhood trauma.

This silk hit different. I walked over to the full-length mirror and watched as I twirled around in circles. Once. Twice. A third time.

I felt utterly beautiful. I felt sexy and empowered. I felt confident and affirmed. I felt, well, proud. I made my way into the living room, excited to show my parents.

I won't lie to you: at first it made my mum visibly uncomfortable, as did many things about the way I presented as a non-binary human at first. Her own healing through fear and internalised transphobia took some time – but it wouldn't be long before she herself bought me silk pyjamas.

Then I went into my backyard to take selfies of me wearing the glamorous set to send to the brand. It was golden hour, the light was gorgeous and I was grateful.

Grateful that in this very moment I no longer had to be that ashamed little boy 'cross-dressing' in private. Grateful that I could stand here, having worked through my shame and trauma, empowered in my sexuality. Empowered in my identity, defying patriarchy and dressing authentically. Who knew I'd find freedom in a silk camisole.

Sexual health resources you might find helpful:

ACON (New South Wales)

acon.org.au

ACON are a truly fantastic Queer community health organisation, based in New South Wales.

headspace (Australia-wide)

headspace.org.au

I recently did some work for headspace, a national organisation focused on youth mental health – not to be confused with the mindfulness app. They're particularly great for young people in need of counselling and care, and are also super LGBTQIA+ friendly.

Lifeline (Australia-wide)

13 11 14 (twenty-four-hour crisis support)

Lifeline provides mental health support, suicide prevention services and emotional assistance, anonymously if preferred, over the phone, face-to-face and online.

Sexual Health Quarters (Australia-wide)

shq.org.au

SHQ is an independent, non-profit organisation providing specialised services in sexual health and relationship wellbeing for all. Head to their website to access the services they offer.

Thorne Harbour Health (Melbourne)

thorneharbour.org

THH provide an excellent, judgement-free space to access Queer healthcare in Melbourne. I found it to be without question the most helpful therapy service of its kind.

Sex-positive influencers to follow on Instagram:

@abbiechatfield

@asti.maree

@brandonkylegoodman

@chantelle_otten_sexologist

@clementine_ford

@comfortableinmyskin

@gspot._

@kathebbs

@lucymneville

@queersextherapy

Affirmation

In this moment, I release any shame attached to sex, sexuality and gender.

I am proud of who I am.
I am proud of the sexuality I am so divinely filled with.

I relish in its power, and reject the shame and guilt that no longer serves me.
It has never served me.

I move in flow with my identity.

A letter on gender

I receive DMs from parents almost daily asking me to write a book themed on gender, and in many ways that would have been the expectation for this book. Since coming out as non-binary two years ago, I have dedicated a whole lot of space to conversations around gender and living beyond the binary. Social media space, podcast space, written space.

The truth is, though, I am still very much on my own gender journey, and there are other humans much further down their journey with non-binary identities, with far greater expertise on the subject than me at present. Humans like Jeffrey Marsh and Alok V Menon. If you are unfamiliar with either of them, I encourage you to look them up and devour both their books and content.

That being said, it would be weird if I didn't cover the biggest sliding-door moment of my life thus far to some capacity. As I've mentioned, I credit the long hours of lockdown for this turning point in my life; it was that blessing of time and space that really allowed me to look inwards and really do the work. So, in an attempt to give you a breather before we jump into another very meaty chapter, I wanted to share some of my thoughts on gender with you.

The first thing to note is that sex and gender are two very separate things that often get confused as the same. When we each enter this world, we are assigned a sex at birth, traditionally declared male or female or intersex, based on the genitals between our legs. In delivery rooms the world over, obstetricians will traditionally announce one of two sentences to eagerly anticipating parents: 'It's a GIRL' or 'It's a BOY'.

An important note here: being intersex is not my lived experience, but people living with intersex variations are constantly overlooked in conversations about sex and gender, even though research tells us that 1.7 percent of the population are born with intersex variations, which is the same number of people born with red hair! For more information and resources on the intersex community, I highly recommend you head over to the Intersex Human Rights Australia website (ihra.org.au).

My mum has told me that during her pregnancy when she heard I was going to be a 'boy', she felt waves of sadness, having hoped that she would be blessed with a daughter. I've heard stories of parents' genuine anguish over the sex of their children. But why is there such universal pressure and expectation placed on humans who have barely opened their eyes to possess a certain gender identity?

This, my darlings, is where gender comes into play and sex assigned at birth is left far behind.

In my very first session with Elise, she described me as someone with more feminine energy than she had seen in even some of her cisgender female clients. She said this existed in me alongside the masculine, creating a combination that went beyond the male/female divide. In many ways, it was this session that led me towards my own journey of gender discovery.

To explain it very simply, I identify as non-binary. To make that make sense, I will first explain to you what a binary system means. The word binary is used when referring to a system that consists of two things. In the case of gender identity, it has for a long time, especially in Western history, been considered to consist of only male and female. But we know of many examples across First Nations and Eastern cultures of gender identities that transcend these rigid binary norms. What's more, people who live with what we understand in Western terms as trans or gender-diverse identities have often been celebrated or lifted up within their communities, seen to possess invaluable insight based on their unique experiences with gender. A few examples include Brotherboys and Sistergirls from First Nations communities in Australia, to two-spirit Native Americans and the 'third gender' Fa'afafine peoples of the Samoan diaspora.

Non-binary means that I, and individuals like me, can't exist within traditional societal categories of man or woman.

Within the non-binary umbrella there is a variation of identities, from gender nonconforming to genderfluid and genderqueer. Gender expression and gender identity are unique to each individual's lived experience, and there's a great deal of nuance to understand here. Let's start by defining those ideas.

Gender expression refers to the ways that a person's behaviour, mannerisms and appearance come to be associated with feminine or masculine gender roles. This is about someone's external presentation (think clothing, hair, make-up, etc.), and these categories often rely on gendered assumptions and stereotypes about how 'men' or 'women' *should* behave in our society.

Gender identity is more of an inward-facing concept about how we understand our own gender. When someone is cisgender, their gender identity correlates with their assigned sex; when they are trans and/or non-binary, their gender differs from their assigned sex. Our gender identity is who we know ourselves to be.

Non-binary humans also sometimes use the term trans to describe themselves, as by definition transgender means not identifying with the sex assigned to you at birth. So within the trans umbrella, you have binary transitions – think Caitlyn Jenner, a rather problematic woman most globally known for a transition many of us witnessed via her family's television show. May I point you in the direction of the exceptional Laverne Cox instead? Thank me later.

In these binary transitions, it can be common to pursue medical intervention, such as hormones and surgery – though not always. An operation or injection does not validate or invalidate someone's gender, but it can do a great deal in helping them to outwardly express their internal sense of self. For non-binary folks, medical interventions are less common, but as with any identity group, there are huge variations between experiences of non-binary identity. Some transitions involve medical intervention with hormones for example, but other people might not tie their non-binary identity to external changes in our bodies. Every non-binary journey is different; this all varies from person to person.

A lot to digest? I know, it was for me too.

You may have noticed that I introduced myself in this book with my pronouns, they/them, just as they're displayed on my Instagram and on the Instagram bios of many humans, both cishet or not. The reason you might have noticed this 'trend' of late is because with an increasing awareness of the complex nature of gender identity comes a rising consciousness that we cannot judge any human by how they present themselves. So by me and others being very clear with our identity and the pronouns we use, there is no room for misgendering. That's when you use pronouns or a form of address that doesn't reflect a person's gender identity.

Not only is misgendering harmful to the trans community – research shows a direct correlation between misgendering and poor mental health, self-harm and suicide – it can also stir up feelings of gender dysphoria in trans people, amplifying their discomfort or distress over the sense of mismatch between their gender identity and their sex. Imagine being perceived and spoken to every single day with language that doesn't reflect the way you identify. You'd feel hurt, invisible, unappreciated and disrespected. The other great benefit of being both vocal and visible with your pronouns is that it shows allyship, and it gives space for those around you to do the same safely.

If you take one thing away from this, I would love for it to be the following: no two people share the same lived experience, but every single person in this world is, in some way, shape or form, either benefiting from or carrying baggage based on their gender.

Get to know the nuanced, intersectional nature of feminism. Become familiar with the fact that feminism must include all women, including trans women, because trans women are women. Know that the journey of a white woman will never be the same as that of an Indigenous or Black woman, or women of colour. We must understand that a trans person doesn't have the same social privilege as a cis person.

Never underestimate the impact that even your micro-expressions of allyship can have on Queer people. Put your pronouns in your bios and email signatures. Use them in team meetings. Wear those rainbow lanyards with pride, pin those pronoun badges to your uniform. Smile at that trans person opposite you in the line at Starbucks. It all goes such a long way and means more to us than you may ever know.

So please, be kind. Lead with empathy and respect, and a knowledge that while you may never understand the lived experience of another, you can still very much stand alongside them with your support and allyship.

No matter the pronouns we use.

5.

Matters of the heart

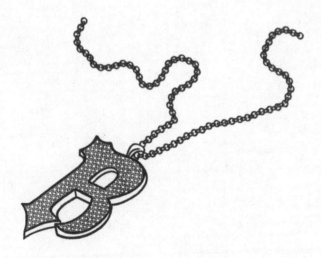

Fucking LOVE, hey? The universal language we all speak. No matter who you are, how old you are, how you identify or where you may be reading this, I could almost bet my life on the fact that you have at some point experienced the dizzying heights of love and the tremendous lows of heartbreak. Matters of the heart are some of the most intense human emotions you'll ever experience. In one swift moment you can go from feeling as though it couldn't possibly get better than 'this', until 'this' becomes 'that' and you're left to feel as though your insides might actually combust.

Ask any healer, spiritual medium or psychic what their number one question is when they have a client sitting opposite them and they will tell you the question almost always centres on love. Think of all the therapists who have sat opposite a wounded human navigating their way out of heartbreak. Unpacking, session by session, the many layers that come with the end of a relationship.

Did you know that:

- Love truly is a drug – in fact, it's just as addictive as cocaine! Studies suggest that the subjective state of 'being in love' is tied to biochemical reactions occurring within the brain involving compounds such as dopamine, oxytocin, vasopressin and serotonin. All of these influence brain regions known to play a role in the development of trust, the generation of pleasure and the signalling of reward. *(The Guardian)*

- 'Butterflies' are real. They're a stress response caused by the excessive amount of adrenaline your body produces when you see the object of your affection. *(Review 42)*
- Broken heart syndrome is a diagnosed condition for people suffering from heartbreak. *(FearlessSoul)*

Why are so many humans constantly searching for the elusive 'one'? If you can literally die of a broken heart, what makes us want to go back to the possibility of feeling love once more? Are we born addicted to love?

A Harvard study conducted over seventy-five years revealed that the main source of happiness in life is romantic love. Their findings concluded that happiness and pleasure in life are derived from love, or the search for love.

If reading this triggers you, you're not alone. Recent studies showed that 33 percent of Australian marriages end in divorce, while countless other relationships fall by the wayside. Another survey from Relationships Australia in 2021 found 42 percent of respondents said that the isolation of lockdowns had negatively impacted their relationship with their partner. Suffice to say, we are as a collective very familiar with heartbreak.

Yet in the midst of this, we're also having a long-overdue cultural conversation about the love we're supposed to have for ourselves.

As I've mentioned, in 2021 I was part of a national campaign titled Self Love Uprising. There were photos of me plastered on billboards and bus stops all over Australia with the words SELF and LOVE spread across my body. It was a career-defining moment and a personal highlight for me, as it brought me closer to so much of my audience. However, it also came with the realisation that so many people have such little love for themselves. Every day I found myself reading messages from humans exclaiming, 'You should be so proud of this self-love campaign, I wish I could love myself.' Those messages broke my heart, because I was all too familiar with that feeling.

The campaign also made me realise that there is a huge variation in people's perception of what 'self-love' means. Somewhere along the line the ideas of self-care and self-love have been confused, and the way we nurture our relationship with ourselves has been lost with the messaging of how we care for ourselves in some form of daily practice. A sheet mask is soothing and all, but let's be honest, it's not going to do much for healing that trauma, darling.

A global report launched by The Body Shop in March 2021 identified a self-love crisis particularly in women, with one in two women feeling more self-doubt than self-love, and 60 percent wishing they had more respect for themselves. The Body Shop Global Self Love Index was a first-of-its-kind study, commissioned to inform a long-term commitment from the brand to use its voice to build self-esteem. I've not been #sponsored to include this data here; I'm sharing it with you because clearly this crisis calls for support and solutions. While these results floored me, they also didn't surprise me. If our relationship with ourselves is informed by our relationships with those around us, it becomes clearer to keep connecting the dots, as we've already started to do in this book.

But where does one even begin?

In this chapter we're going to unpack all of it. From love and loss to grief and healing and love, once more, and ending on the most important of all loves – self-love.

✦

Before we do our deep dive, let me invite you back into the space that I find myself in while I'm writing this. I'm sitting on the balcony of the home of my partner Archie's parents in the Mornington Peninsula of Victoria's coastline.

I'm appreciating how much of a full-circle moment this is, feeling incredibly content at my in-laws' place, while my beautiful partner swims across the street. Here I am, two weeks shy of my thirty-fourth birthday, in the healthiest relationship I've ever had.

Archie and I 'met' during the last Victorian lockdown, on an otherwise ordinary Thursday evening on the couch. The profile picture and description on their online dating profile caught my eye, and before I knew it we were a match. After an hour's worth of robust, effortless conversation, we exchanged numbers.

Archie and I would go on to spend three weeks – weeks that felt like months in lockdown – getting to know each other intimately. All without being in the same room, the Melbourne–Geelong border dividing us. What we didn't then fully appreciate was that would be our greatest blessing: when you have what feels like unlimited time to just get to know someone, you get real deep, real quick.

By the time our first IRL date happened, I knew instantly that this was not to be a fleeting affair. By our second date, we sat in a park, discussing weddings and saving for surrogacy. Fast-forwarding to the present day, we now live together. Who knew lockdown would usher in not only my authentic identity but also my soulmate?

Single me would have felt pangs of longing reading descriptions of the above scenario. So, if you reading this are currently uncoupled, let me assure you it was not always this way.

Do you remember your first real love? I was twenty years old when I had mine. I'd been out as gay for twelve months and was navigating my way through a new season of life. I'd been sleeping with a boy the same age as me. We've remained great friends, so I'm sure he won't mind me saying this. At his core he was sweet and kind, but alongside his cool, nonchalant demeanour was a very honest declaration that he couldn't commit to anything other than sex.

So over the course of a nine-month period, I would willingly collect the crumbs he occasionally offered me. A train ride home from work side by side. A sushi date here and there. Before long this escalated to boozy pashes on the dance floor that typically resulted in us both hopping into a cab and heading back to his house, to have sex in the granny flat he lived in. We'd have many conversations on those pillows, but seldom getting deep enough to allow for any real intimacy. I would leave in the morning to make my way back home, hoping and wishing for more.

Then there was Ben.

Ben worked at my local Video Ezy. (Remember those?) My brother and I had developed a weekly ritual of renting DVDs to watch, and one night there I noticed a tall, boyishly handsome human standing behind the counter. I'd seen him at the store a million times before, surely, but I guess I'd never really looked at him.

'If I pay for my fees now, does that fifty percent discount apply?' I asked, enquiring about the sign I saw on the counter.

'Don't worry, I can just wipe your overdue fees,' he said with a smile.

It was in that moment I noticed his eyes light up and I wondered if he, too, was gay.

Geelong is a very small place, and short of three months later I was sitting across from this human, Ben, on what I later discovered was a group date. We had a mutual friend in common and she very casually organised for us to all meet for a drink, knowing that Ben had a crush on me. I wasn't particularly into the idea at the time because I was still longing for Mr Fuckboy.

About a month later, I had given Fuckboy the flick. So I went out on the town with my cousin, to drink my wounded heart away. It was somewhere towards the end of the night that Ben popped up beside me. I was pleasantly surprised he was there; I didn't remember him being THIS CUTE. So we exchanged numbers. When I tell you things moved quickly, things moved quickly, and seven weeks later we said I love you to one another. A night I will never forget.

Do you remember the first time you said 'I love you' to another human and really, really meant it? It felt as though every single butterfly in the animal kingdom had decided to congregate within my abdomen, and my heart pulsed outside of my chest. My palms were sweaty and I felt increasingly dizzy as Ben and I held each other's face in our hands. If this is what love was going to feel like, I thought, sign me the fuck up.

In retrospect, Ben and I were doomed to end from the beginning. I was a hopeless romantic. Ben, on the other hand, was a very pragmatic human. He didn't believe in Hollywood, or destiny, or soulmates. He didn't care for marriage and I don't think he particularly wanted to have children. Two things I have always longed for. Ben was white and I was brown skinned, and while not all mixed-race relationships end, it would be remiss of me to not acknowledge the difference in our lived experiences and the role that race played in our relationship. Ben was also five years my senior and fiercely independent, quite the opposite approach to my innate desire for co-dependency.

To give you a sense of how I express my love, I'll tell you this story. Shortly after Ben and I had started to date, I wandered into an op shop with my brother. When my brother went to pay for his purchase, I leaned over to rest on the counter. Staring into the glass cabinet underneath, I saw a fine chain necklace with a diamante-encrusted B pendant in a sea of trashy jewellery. I showed it to my brother, exclaiming, 'This is destiny. I'm going to buy this necklace and when Ben and I become official, I'm going to wear it.'

The morning after Ben and I said I love you to each other, I fastened that clasp on the back of my neck and there the necklace hung. For eighteen months. I was so proud of this human and our love that I wanted to wear his initials around my neck, not because I was a piece of his property or he had any kind of ownership of me, but because in that moment it felt as though he was the only person who really knew me, just as Taylor Swift once sang. I wore the necklace every single day, until the morning that it broke.

We had recently moved to London together and, truth be told, our relationship was on its last legs. I remember waking up and noticing something was missing around my neck. The moment I saw the necklace's broken chain in our sheets I felt sick. My superstitious Serbian intuition declared that this was a bad omen. I put the necklace on my bedside and told Ben I'd have to take it to a jeweller to be repaired. Except that I never got around to it and three weeks later, I packed my suitcase to move out of our house. Alone.

I cried on the phone to Mum, who was begging me to just come back home to Geelong. However, at that moment I had decided that my breakup with Ben wouldn't define my London journey. What hurt most for me was not the breakup itself, but rather the way in which our relationship ended. Think horrible screaming matches and a betrayal of trust.

Spoiler alert: time can, as they say, heal many wounds, and personal growth helps too. Ben and I are now great friends. But at that time I'd wondered, how could I, the son of two humans who love each other so much and have loved me so much, be sitting here as the victim? This was not meant to be my narrative, and yet it was.

'The relationships your parents have become the scaffolding of what you'd expect to have or look for in your own relationships,' Elise told me. Those relationship models will unconsciously play out in our own lives. Toxic family dynamic? An absent parent? Abuse? Infidelity? Addiction? Our impressionable brains soak all of this up, and while phrases like 'daddy issues' get thrown around a lot, Elise says they are clichés for a reason.

We might hate to admit it, but if most of us look deeply enough within ourselves and at our relationship history, we can find reference points for comparison with the types of love that were modelled by our parents. We either repeat history and do exactly as our parents did, or we make the choice to steer our relationships in a total opposite direction. Elise says that our parents' relationships and the relationships we have with our parents form the foundational scaffolding for our attachment styles and love languages.

What is a love language?

We all give and receive love in very different ways. Marriage counsellor Dr Gary Chapman developed the framework of the five 'love languages' to codify some overarching similarities he noticed in individuals' expressions of love through his research and extensive work in the field. One bestselling book and an appearance on Oprah's show later, and BOOM, you've got the whole world onto something.

Here is a breakdown of Dr Chapman's love languages and what they mean in practice. At dinner parties I love playing the game of 'What's your love language?', and I almost always explain to people that each of us at some point will speak all five of the love languages. With that said, there is often a hierarchy for each human, and what's even more interesting is that your hierarchy for giving love can vary from your hierarchy of receiving love. The way you best receive love can differ entirely from the way you express it. For example, I love giving gifts, but receiving gifts doesn't rate so highly for me.

Words of affirmation

This love language involves expressing affection through spoken words, praise or appreciation. When this is someone's primary love language, they value words above all else. They respond well to encouragement and feedback, they're likely a sucker for an uplifting quote, love notes and cute text messages. Words of affirmation is my number one for both the way I give and receive love.

Quality time

Love and affection are expressed for someone with this love language through undivided attention. This person feels loved if you are present and focused on them. So honey, put the phone down, turn off the telly, make eye contact, and be an active listener. People with this as their primary love language are after quality versus quantity. My partner Archie expresses love through quality time in a big way, so active listening is a practice I'm constantly working on.

Physical touch

Spoiler alert – this doesn't always mean sex. This human feels loved through physical affection. Aside from sex, they feel loved when their partner holds their hand, touches their arm, or gives them a cuddle at the end of the day; they simply want to be close to their partner physically. My dad is a physical-touch human: whether that touch is from my mother or a friend, he's a hugger, he's a kisser of cheeks and foreheads. Physical touch is also my close second. Because apples and trees, ya know?

Acts of service

For acts of service, a person feels loved and appreciated when someone does nice things for them. This can vary from emptying out the dishwasher to driving your car to the servo to fill up the tank so that you don't have to.

They love when people do little things for them and are often found doing acts of service for others. My mother is an acts-of-service kinda gal. She at times struggles with articulating her emotions but when it comes to showing those around her love, her acts of service are unmatched.

Gifts

Gift-giving is symbolic of love and affection for humans with this love language. They treasure not only the gift itself but also the time and effort the gift-giver put into it. In fact, I'd go as far as to say that the gift alone needn't be big or flashy or expensive; it is the thought that often counts most. People with this love language, like my brother, often remember every little gift they have received from their loved ones because it makes such an impact on them.

Have a think about what your hierarchy of love languages are; order them from 1 to 5. Then ask the loved ones around you. The most crucial thing about this exercise is that it involves an understanding that no two or more people need to speak the same love language in order to have a successful relationship, but understanding each other's language is key, as is being able to communicate your own.

Back to the main story here: the ways our relationship patterns have been informed by our parents. After my conversations with Elise, and a long period of self-reflection, my raised levels of consciousness revealed many hard truths.

Remember when my therapist made me aware of the fact that my family had never really instilled boundaries in our house? This set a precedent for the way in which I would be treated across all my romantic relationships, and my friendships too. Let me give you a quick relationship history recap.

There was Ben, my first love; my experiences with Ben began my self-love journey. Then there was Brendan, my first real adult love. I met Brendan when I was twenty-four, during what I would later describe as our 'summer of love'. He was the first person I ever imagined marrying and starting a family with, but this relationship taught me that sometimes people do just grow apart and fall out of love with another. Brendan is one of the best people I've ever known, and is now one of my best friends.

In the relationship I was in before I met Archie, I learnt more about myself and about the world than in any other; it was a dramatic time of highs and lows, and a relationship that separated me from who I was at my core and what I really wanted. But time once more makes way for healing, and while that person and I aren't as close as I am with Ben and Brendan, I will always be grateful that the universe put us on the same path, because there is a reason and a lesson in everything.

The common denominator in almost all of my past romantic relationships was that on some level there was a mistreatment of my worth, identity, kindness and trust. I was once described as a doormat anyone could walk over; another boyfriend once described me as tofu. Tofu has no flavour and adapts to the flavours of whatever you cook it with; that's how he found me, easy to manipulate to suit the lifestyle and choices of his liking. You know what, I wouldn't have disagreed with him! In almost every romantic relationship, I've changed aspects of myself to suit my partner – not that they ever asked me to, but when you know, you know. These changes ranged from different haircut styles to dressing in a more masculine manner, from eating different foods to changing up my social life, often pushing away the people who were closest to me. I often heard questions like, 'Where has the old Deni gone?'

When I dug a little deeper into why that might be, it came down to my lack of boundaries. If we go even deeper than that, we start to recognise that a lack of boundaries comes from a lack of self-love – and if we dig even deeper, self-love is fundamentally the confident ability to respect and honour your authentic self. Not compromising the integrity of your identity is the only way one can ever truly live authentically.

Easier said than done, you say? Perhaps. But we set boundaries for things we love all the fucking time. Let me give you an example.

You buy a new car. It's THE CAR. You've saved hard for it, you shopped around to get the best deal, to get the right colour and that fabulous vanity mirror that's so well lit you can already imagine the Friday night lipstick applications. The sound system is major, and the interiors? Fuck, the interiors are mint. So imagine, one night, you pick up your sister and tell her you're taking her for a spin in your new wheels, filled with pride to show her this investment. Your sister opens the door, commenting first on her disdain for the car's colour. As she sits herself down on the cream leather seats you can see her trousers are stained. Her Converses have mud on them and she proceeds to throw her bag carelessly onto the floor of the passenger side, its contents spilling out as it lands. She leans over to pick them up and opens a bag of chips because 'she's starving', and before you know it crumbs go everywhere, even though you told her there's no food allowed in the new car.

How would you react?

I can almost guarantee you would tell her off, you'd back your choice of colour and you'd continue to stand your ground, pointing out her dirty shoes and insisting she not eat in your brand-new car.

See, the thing is, you love this car. You worked hard to buy this car. You wanted to share this moment of financial and emotional investment with her, but she challenged your boundaries and disrespected you.

So riddle me this. If we can speak with such confidence when it comes to material, inanimate objects, setting boundaries and communicating the minutiae of any single one that is overstepped, why do we have such difficulty doing the same for ourselves?

My expression of self-love has been a rather complicated journey over the years. Those who know me intimately would tell you that I have always been an outwardly 'confident' human. Confident in many ways. Confident of my worth in a professional capacity. Confident in my penchant for performing. After the initial awkward teething stages of my new Queer life, that confidence translated to boys, sex and dating. If you were standing opposite me at the club and I found you attractive, chances are I would have made my way over to you to shoot my shot. Life's too short, and so often confidence will get you everywhere.

However, confidence can be mistaken for self-love. Some of the most confident people I've ever met have also had the lowest levels of self-esteem and love for themselves. Defence mechanisms are funny little things. Throughout childhood I developed a very thick skin; no matter how lost I felt or how bullied I was at school, I was never going to let people sense my pain. From the outside I appeared confident: I shone bright and danced to the beat of my own drum. But inside, make no mistake, I was insecure as fuck, a self-loathing human with low self-worth. It wasn't until my first breakup in London that I really started to think about why this was and how I could rebuild the relationship with myself.

The pain, vulnerability and fragility of my first breakup were only further compounded by the fact that it was unfolding halfway across the world, away from the support networks of my family and best friends, who so desperately wanted to be there for me. Instead, there I was, a twenty-two-year-old, in an unfamiliar city where I was in many ways alone but could also truly be anyone I wanted to be.

The moment I decided to dedicate my London years to myself, everything changed. I found great power. I threw myself into work, interning and assisting and freelancing and soaking up every morsel of every opportunity that was thrown my way. I moved into a share house. I lived with strangers for the first time in my life. I could wear whatever the fuck I wanted, without anyone telling me I was too feminine. I was single, in London. You'd better believe I was going to make the most of it.

Breakups fucking suck. Until suddenly, one day, they suck less. And less. And less. And then, at a time you least expect, you realise you haven't thought about your ex at all, and you pat yourself on the shoulder. Then two more days pass, and three, and four and five, and you realise you've not thought about them all week. And so you continue, living your life, until a whole month has passed and the thought of your ex hasn't crossed your mind.

Every feeling is temporary, even heartbreak.

Elise's breakup tips

Tip 1: Acknowledge your grief

Let yourself be sad for the loss of that person. Let yourself feel their absence, while also asking yourself how much of the feeling that you have about their absence, for example sadness, was possibly there even when they were around or before that. Analyse what you're feeling and what you can do to fill their absence with positive self-care.

Deni's notes: Don't turn to the vices that your friends and angsty television shows may encourage you to reach for. No amount of drugs or alcohol or meaningless sex will make you feel better. Although you'll likely want to reach for that bottle of tequila, I can assure you it will leave you feeling emptier than you did before. Put the bottle down and go run a bath, hun. I promise you'll thank me for it.

Tip 2: Cut all connection with your ex

This is going to be hard. Make your life absent of your ex by removing all reminders. Elise goes as far as to suggest the following method she has put in place for herself post-breakup. Write a list of all the negative things that came from that relationship, the ways in which you felt, the hurt that occurred and anything else that makes you aware of the fact that this breakup is for the best and that the relationship was not serving you. Keep this list within arm's reach – put it by your bed, for example – for as long as you need to so that it can serve as a reminder that you deserve better than this. Some relationships cannot become friendships after a breakup; in these circumstances, removing reminders of your ex in your life will be helpful for you to move on.

Deni's notes: The list method is worth its weight in gold. I've done this for almost every breakup and I promise you that, in time, you'll read back on that list and wonder why the fuck you put up with that shit.

Tip 3: 'Revenge manifestation'

A breakup is the perfect time to reinvent yourself. Rebrand, honey; think Kourtney and Kim Kardashian energy. Get your mojo back, lean into the essence and spirit of who you are and make your wish list. Your wish list should include the life you want to live and, when you're ready, the ways in which you want future relationships to feel. Call out what you rightfully deserve. It may sound woo-woo, but it works. With that said: don't just make change for change's sake! Give yourself permission to bounce back through acts of self-love and authentic expression.

Deni's notes: Get that haircut, wear that outfit your ex said they never liked, explore new spaces that they never wanted to with you. Now is your time to shine. Once you are settled within your reinvention process, manifest the fuck out of the life and love that you deserve. I know you're rolling your eyes at me, but I promise, these are clichés for a reason.

My post-breakup reinvention didn't come all at once. It happened over a long period, by way of many magical Sundays. I used to call Sundays my 'dates with myself' or 'Deni Dates'. They started with a curiosity to discover London in my new-found single status and developed into a fundamental part of my self-love journey. Those Sundays laid the foundations for my relationship with myself.

I would set my alarm, no matter how hungover I might have been from all the dancing the night before, and I looked forward to choosing an outfit to impress only myself. I would choose a borough in London I had not yet visited and I would walk. I found quiet paths and canals to stroll along, and where there was little to nobody around to watch me, I would dance, with great vigour, to the songs of Lady Gaga's *The Fame Monster*. That album brought me joy and, with every beat, I grew closer to myself.

I shopped in vintage stores and at H&M. I took myself to the cinema, a highly underrated solo activity. I even took myself to dinner; sometimes I'd bring a book and other times I would just sit and watch the bustling crowds go by. I treasured this time where I was truly alone and, if I'm honest, I often miss it. The thoughts and endless hope that got me through what could've been a very dark moment actually moved me towards the light.

On Sunday afternoons I would daydream of where my life might take me. To a career in fashion, to accomplishments fulfilled and healthy relationships relished. I didn't know what manifesting was back then, but in retrospect I can see that what I was doing on those Sundays was unwittingly manifesting so much of the future course of my life.

My friends used to make fun of my solo Sundays, asking questions like, 'How can you go to the cinema by yourself, doesn't that make you feel sad?' In truth, I felt sad for them – sad that they couldn't stand the silence of their own company. But I find it interesting that spending quality time with yourself can sometimes be considered as lonely or even *gasp* *sad* by others.

That's not to say I haven't had my own share of loneliness. I've felt it often and for various reasons in my life. Sometimes it's when I'm most surrounded by people that I've felt the loneliest. In my experience, however, the key has been to become incredibly comfortable in your company. When you truly love your own company, you will seldom feel alone.

Why do we fear such loneliness? As children we grew anxious of being alone, not being hugged when we needed it most, not being one of the chosen kids in the sandpit, not sitting at the right lunch table, or not being invited to the cool parties, etc. I mean, the list is long. As young adults, the feeling of isolation creeps in when we're presented with the choice of defining our career path regardless of whether it's something we even want, when we submit an application for that summer job, or discover that all our friends are coupling up and you haven't even kissed anybody yet.

As for our adult lives, we live in a world that declares any single human over a certain age 'sad'. There are marketing campaigns and dating apps rolled out every year to help you FIND THE ONE. The potential for loneliness is limitless, and that's exacerbated by the messaging we receive from the culture at large, which blames us for being alone, and tells us we need to pay money to fix it.

But there's no easy solution. And I'd suggest that we need to reconfigure the way we speak about loneliness. There aren't nearly enough social movements to celebrate the power of being alone: the power of working on yourself, in sitting in the shadows, to truly fall in love with who you are. Don't wait around for someone else to complete you, honey. You're a whole damn person.

What happened to me through many years of healing, a healing that is constant and infinite in its motion, was that I arrived at an understanding that there is no such thing as 'the old me'. My mindset was different, and I was living with a renewed sense of joy and was ready to find strength within me, but the reality is that that strength had always lain dormant within me. While I knew that Wounded Deni would always exist within the history of my heart, I paved a new road for growth. A releasing of the old, with great reverence, to make way for the new. Because I was finally ready to be true to myself. Not without struggle, of course.

As I've said, therapy was where it all truly began for little broken Deni. My first dalliance with the therapist's couch came after my breakup with Ben. I was back home in Geelong and suddenly remembered every street corner and bar we had ever walked on, talked in, kissed on and fought in. The number one takeaway I got from my therapist was the following advice:

'Think of your life like a ruler, Deni: over the course of your life, different people will walk in and walk out. Some will stay for a centimetre, others may stay for five, or ten, or two or twenty, but no matter how little or long they stay, they all make you grow.'

My second stint in therapy was during my years in Sydney, when I was into my third relationship.

After one tremendously difficult weekend, I was left locked out of my apartment at 5 am. My keys were with my boyfriend who had stormed out on me a half-hour earlier, on the way home from the club. I didn't want to make the eight-minute walk over to his house to retrieve them, because pride and stubbornness are a combo no one asks for. It was too early to call any of my friends or family, so I made my way to a nearby park in Paddington.

I sat in that park and stress-smoked cigarettes, one by one. I despised cigarettes until I met him and his gaggle of gay friends; we spent most of our weekend nights out, the evenings punctuated by gossip and D&Ms as we chain-smoked in the smoker's area aka 'Trash Alley' at Arq. It was either get with it or get left behind, so I gave in.

As I was crying into my third cigarette, a voice inside told me to google Lifeline. I'd seen the ads before, but I'd never thought I'd find myself in a scenario where I would actually need a service like that in my life. Can you hear the stigma attached to my thoughts? 'You come from a family of love, Deni. Why would you need to turn to a stranger at a helpline?'

I called the number and the angel on the other end of the phone talked me through and out of a true mental spiral. She made me aware that I was shaking not because I had been locked out in the cold. I was shaking because I was worried about my boyfriend and the problems in our relationship. She advised me to go seek counselling to give me an appropriate emotional toolkit.

I made the call that Monday. Then I walked into my therapist's office the following week. The main takeaway I got from my six-month stint with them went as follows:

'Deni, you have an inherent desire to fix people. It's the reason you've dated variations of the same person over and over and it stems from your childhood. Your parents raised you to believe that love cures all. For this very reason, no matter what trials and tribulations a relationship presents you with, you believe that your love will always conquer. Even when that love is detrimental to your wellbeing and crosses the lines of the boundaries you've yet to set.'

It was this sentence that stood out to me. *Your parents raised you to believe that love cures all.*

Let's assess the evidence, shall we?

Yes, my parents had a happier-than-most marriage. However, their origin story did not come without drama. Or trauma, for that matter. Theirs was a story of village folklore that was so famous, we often said it should be adapted for the silver screen. They met and 'fell in love' at the age of nine years old. Mum was the good girl from the somewhat poorer side of the tracks. Dad was the ultimate bad boy from the slightly wealthier side of the tracks.

They dated in secret, and at sixteen, were separated because my mum had to make her way to this place they called 'The Lucky Country'. They kept in touch via letters for five whole years, until Dad proposed in one of them. When Mum, aged twenty, packed her bags to head back to Serbia to marry her 'one true love', her mother was not so approving. Dad had developed a reputation as a ladies' man, and my grandmother wouldn't approve of this union unless it was on her terms.

I'm giving you only top-line information here, but essentially their parents couldn't settle on a wedding date. The wedding was called off and my mother locked in her room. My grandmother slapped her (because remember, 'ethnic discipline') for the way she had embarrassed their family, and informed her that she would be flying back to Melbourne the next morning. Not even a goodbye to my father was permitted.

So, like something out of a Danielle Steel novel, my mother managed to convince her favourite auntie to let her out briefly to say farewell to my dad. Upon my mum's arrival at his house, my dad locked them in his room and declared to my mother that tomorrow they would wed, at the town hall, with no formal ceremony and no family present. Because THEIR LOVE WAS ALL THEY NEEDED. My mum got married in a white silk jumpsuit she used to wear nightclubbing. After they said their 'I dos', her mother didn't speak to them for three months.

I'd listen to this story, time and time again, for most of my life, oohing and aahing in awe. Is it any wonder I put up with so much drama in my own relationships? I thought drama was a required ingredient for the making of successful unions. It was for my parents. It was for the couples on *Days of Our Lives*, *Melrose Place* and *The Bold and the Beautiful*, and for countless other Hollywood rom-coms that informed my mind for OVER A DECADE.

Drama is not a necessary ingredient; it's a toxic roller-coaster that, by my late twenties, I wanted to get off. What my second therapist made me realise was that love is simply not enough.

⟡

Do you watch *RuPaul's Drag Race*? If you do, you'll be familiar with Mama Ru's words that close each episode: 'IF YOU CAN'T LOVE YOURSELF, HOW IN THE HELL YOU GON' LOVE SOMEBODY ELSE? CAN I GET AN AMEN UP IN HERE!'

It wasn't until I started seeing my third therapist that I realised the number of times I'd squealed amen at the screen, never truly listening to what Mama Ru had said. In my first session with this therapist – having returned to Melbourne after finally ending my last toxic relationship – I had the revelation about my boundary-free existence. I knew I needed to dedicate real quality time to heal and to find myself before I could even contemplate loving another human again.

True healing begins when we sit in the shadows. I started to reconnect with the things I used to love and I invested time in the friendships that I had all too quickly neglected. I started working out and being creative and experimenting with my fashion choices and being as bold as ever. The people around me described this season of my life as one in which they finally 'had the real me back'. I taught myself to set boundaries, first with my parents and brother.

Relaying those therapists' conversations with my family was challenging at first. No one wants to hear that their parenting style hadn't given their children adequate preparation for living in the big, bad world. I made peace with their ways and informed my parents that, going forward, I would be exercising my own way of setting boundaries, even encouraging them to do the same. I set my boundaries in my friendships, with my extended family and social media and work colleagues, and suddenly everything just started to click.

Then I met Elise, who taught me about 'shadow work' (more about this later). She taught me about getting comfortable with sitting in the darkness in order to work your way towards the light. I met Elise five weeks before we went into that very first lockdown in March 2020, and it is in large part thanks to her that I began to set up the framework for the biggest season of self-development my soul would experience. Lockdowns gave us time, a gift we often take for granted. While we can't get that time back, and lord knows none of us wants to, a period of solitude is always a good time to start the healing.

As I sat there one afternoon in lockdown, I remembered out of the blue some sage advice passed on to small-town girl Whitney Port by fashion designer legend Diane von Furstenberg in the reality TV show *The City*. The show chronicled Whitney's move to New York City and her job in fashion PR with the iconic DVF.

Towards the finale of season one, when Whitney is having fuckboy problems of her own, Diane turns to her and says,

'Whitney, you must remember that in life, the most important relationship you will ever have is the one with yourself.'

In that moment, I made a promise to myself – and to DVF – that I would never let myself down, and that no matter what the road ahead had in store for me, I had my own back, first, foremost and always.

So, as we draw to this chapter's end, I want you to think about the following questions.

 Over to you, darling

Growing up

- How have the relationships around you, particularly that of your parents, informed and influenced your ability to love and be loved?
- Was the primary relationship you observed growing up a positive one? Was it healthy? Based on respect and trust and safety?
- Have the relationships you've had been informed by trauma you've observed around you, based on societal norms and expectations or problematic tropes in the media? Imma keep it real with you here: think about Disney, think about Hollywood. How did watching these stories inform your impressionable mind about relationships?

Your relationship history

- Have the relationships you've had thus far served your soul for the better?
- Can you, hand on heart, look back at the emotional inventory of all your past relationships and say that you

feel they taught you something, that you've grown and no matter the love lost you feel better for having had them?

- Have you set adequate boundaries in your relationship so as not to compromise the core of who you are? Let's get specific, hun: are you asking for your partner's approval, and if you are, is it because you want to or *feel* you have to?

Your relationship with yourself

- On a scale of one to five, what is your relationship with yourself like?
- Do you actually like yourself?
- Is the relationship you have with yourself a strong one? Do you put effort into making this relationship work, as you would any other kind of relationship?
- Do you enjoy your own company, or do you dread time spent alone? Are you constantly trying to fill the space with noise or things or people? Are you able to sit and be and relish in those moments of solitude?
- Do you have unconditional love for yourself – who you are at the core of your being?
- When was the last time you looked in the mirror and said, 'I love you'?

Here's an affirmation I'd love to encourage you to say out loud, to yourself, in the mirror. Go inwards and look deep within your soul.

Here's your affirmation:

I AM STRONG
I AM KIND
I AM BEAUTIFUL
I AM WORTHY
I AM PROUD OF THE HUMAN I AM
I AM LOVED
I LOVE YOU
AND I WILL ALWAYS LOVE YOU
EVEN WHEN IT'S HARD TO

A lot to digest? I know, darling; trust me, I know. Can we take a moment to pat ourselves on the back for reaching the end of another chapter. *Insert woo chants here.* I know I am. I'm proud of us. Be proud of you!

Now let's celebrate with a dance break!

Dance break

'Stronger' – Kelly Clarkson
We're going to kick things off with one of my favourite empowering breakup anthems. I don't care what anyone says; there is a Kelly Clarkson song for every emotion and the messaging of this song will simply never date. Scream along to Kelly and know that no matter how much pain all the relationship trauma has given you, it's here to make you motherfuckin' stronger, BITCH.

After you've listened to Kelly, I want to take you to a place of rebirth and new beginnings. Remember how Elise suggested we all have opportunities to reinvent ourselves post-breakup? The same can be said for any moment – even now. Embrace it and be emboldened by it. Let's listen to:

'Unwritten' – Natasha Bedingfield (Acoustic Version)

The theme song to the TV show *The Hills*, this is truly one of the most 'main character energy' anthems of all time. It was, however, this slow version of the song, from the show's finale, that pierced my heart wide open. Listen to the lyrics, which are all about writing the next chapters of the story of your life. Because it is never too late to start this journey; healing, when led by intention, is always a good idea.

Wear your own damn name

On my thirty-third birthday, one of my favourite aunties came over to drop off a present. She and I have always been very close, but after I came out as gay and later as non-binary, our relationship went through its own transition of sorts. Having had my safety and wellbeing front of mind, my auntie's maternal and protective nature would often kick in and, much like my own mother, it took some time for her to accept my authentic identity. With change often comes fear, though I knew that her heart has always and will always be in the right place. My auntie and I have always spoken different love languages: she's an 'acts of service' kinda of human, and on this particular birthday, she said more to me with one touching gesture than words ever could.

She came over for a celebratory drink and placed a small pink box in front of me at the dinner table. For context it was the longest I had ever been single (about two and a half years), with not one piece of 'relationship jewellery' adorning my body in that time.

As I opened the small box, I noticed a flash of gold. I pulled out a fine gold chain. Hanging at its centre was my name, spelled out in gold. I hung it in front of me and squealed with glee. 'You got me a nameplate necklace, just like Carrie's.'

I had been obsessed with Carrie Bradshaw from the moment I discovered *Sex and the City*, and my auntie knew how much I loved her style. 'I'm so proud of the journey you've been on this year, and you should be too,' she said to me as I admired the piece of jewellery.

I realised that over the course of my adult life I had never so much as even thought to wear my initials with pride, yet at the birth of every relationship would jump at the opportunity to display my partners' names for the world to see. For many of us, we are comfortable making public declarations about who we love and what we believe in. Whether it's a designer logo, band merch, a badge declaring we've been vaxxed or the jersey of a football team we follow, why are we so ready to cheer for everyone else but ourselves?

I turned to my auntie and said, 'You know what, it's about time I wear my own damn name around my neck.' (Taylor Swift, I give you permission to take that sentence and turn it into a song lyric!)

In that moment, I knew I was ready to finally declare my love for myself. My auntie had given me a beautiful gift, rich in symbolism, and, likely without her even realising it, the necklace became another light-switch moment for me, a gift that I will forever cherish.

Affirmation

Universe, I thank you in advance for blessing me with the
gift of love.
The gift to love and of being loved.

I call out the love I deserve.
A love that honours me the way I love and honour
myself.

I am surrounded by love and am grateful for its
presence.

6.

The hustle

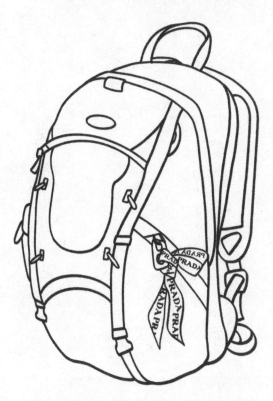

When I was five years old, I wanted to be a stripper. I'd just watched the scene in the movie *Flashdance* where the lead character Alex dances on a chair, bathed in pouring water falling from the ceiling. I mean, 'What a Feeling' indeed. I remember running through my cousins' living room, dancing, exclaiming to a house full of traditional wogs that I was going to be a stripper. They thought it was the funniest thing ever and exploded into roars of laughter.

When I was six, I thought I might like to be a lawyer. This burst of inspiration came from another movie I saw. I don't remember its title but it starred a woman who commanded the attention of the courtroom by simply talking. I fucking love to talk, I could talk under water. Lawyer Deni? Sign me up! Then I learned how many years of schooling it requires to become a lawyer and that desire quickly faded – and I mean, have you seen the levels of studying Kim was doing to pass the bar in the new Kardashians series? Not for me, babes.

It wasn't until I was thirteen that I realised fashion was to be my calling. I had lived and breathed fashion from as early as four, but I didn't know it was a 'job' you could actually do. I thought it was a fantasy career that only rich white people like the Forresters and Spectras from *The Bold and the Beautiful* could have. I stumbled across an episode of the SBS docuseries *Masters of Style* that profiled John Galliano, the problematic, wildly talented fashion visionary who was then creative director of Christian Dior. John came from humble beginnings in Gibraltar and, with little to no financial backing, became the talk of the fashion set. That story lit a fire inside my belly.

I always had a 'life plan'. From as early as five and six, I would spend countless hours daydreaming about what I wanted my life to look like. As I saw that series, I could almost taste my fashion career ahead. There was never a Plan B or a 'real job' fallback plan. If John Galliano and Jean Paul Gaultier and Gianni Versace and Michael Kors could do it, then so could I.

I discovered fashion magazines at around the same time. I bought my first copy of *Vogue Australia* with lunch money from Mum. A girlfriend and I had broken the rules and nipped down to the corner store down the street to buy lunch. My friend made her choice between Doritos and Smith's chips, while my eagle eyes spotted a magazine called *Vogue* on the newsstand. On the cover was the pop star of the moment, Holly Valance, her eyes smoky with brown shadow and her body wrapped in a nude ribbon-like dress. It was Tom Ford for Gucci, and remains one of my favourite Aussie fashion moments.

I picked up the magazine and could almost smell the glamour in its pages. It cost $7.95 and I had ten dollars in my pocket, so I bought the magazine and a Cherry Ripe and made my way back to school. I hid the magazine in my locker so that the boys wouldn't see it and make fun of me. As soon as I got home, I took it home with me and pored over every single detail of every single page, more times than I could even count. From the editor's letter right through to the stockist index at the back, I was intoxicated by this world of fashion that felt so out of reach.

I later discovered *Harper's Bazaar*, and each month, I would ask my mother to buy both magazines for me during our weekly grocery shop. Fourteen dollars a month seemed like a huge amount of money at the time but ever the supportive mum, she would often come home to surprise me with it, tucked in a supermarket bag.

Sometimes I would cut out my favourite pieces from the mags and stick them into a scrapbook, learning to curate and develop my fashion eye. I wrote show reviews in Microsoft Word and trend reports to stick alongside my findings. I was, in my own adolescent way, editing my own magazine. I still have that scrapbook and I once took it into the office when I became the fashion editor of *Cosmopolitan Australia*.

It was also at that impressionable time in my early teens that I became obsessed with designer brands and the logos that adorned their pieces. Their price tags blew my mind. How anyone could afford to spend a thousand dollars on a pair of shoes was beyond me – but rather than feel excluded from the world of luxury fashion, those price tags encouraged me to aspire for more.

What did you want to be when you grew up?

Remember how you'd get asked that by adults as you grew up? Or maybe they didn't ask. Maybe they didn't instil in you the belief system that you could be 'something' when you grow up. Maybe you came from a family that didn't work at all. Maybe you came from a family that had predetermined your career path for you. Or maybe you came from a working-class family that worked to put food on the table.

My parents worked a lot when I was a kid; to this day they still work an almost seven-day week, as did/do most of the migrant relatives around me. Research suggests that, on average, we will spend 90,000 hours of our lives working. That's a third of a person's life, and yet so many humans feel sick at the sound of their alarms beckoning them to rise each morning and make their way to the jobs that employ them. The jobs that take them away from their lives in order to allow them to afford to live. Kind of fucked up, right?

I did a poll on my Instagram about this very topic. Forty percent of my audience don't like what they do for a living, while 60 percent say that they genuinely do. Eighty percent work only one job while the remaining twenty juggle more, which could include a side hustle or simply a secondary, or even third, source of income. Sixty percent of my audience values the concept of having a career, while 40 percent simply work as a means to an end. A large number feel excluded by the topic of career, asking if 'being a mum was considered a full-time job?'

One message in particular still rings in my ears. It was sent to me by a mother in her late thirties, who said that when she was younger she loved the idea of having her own career, but life simply hadn't allowed for that journey. I didn't know how to respond to her message and so I said what I believed to be true. It is never too late, my darling. Never too late.

Famous cook Julia Child released her first book at the age of fifty. Prolific comic book writer Stan Lee was nearly forty when he published *The Fantastic Four*. Renowned designer Vera Wang didn't enter the fashion industry until she was forty, and TV royalty Oprah Winfrey didn't get her big break until she was thirty-two.

If you feel as if your time has passed or you are running along that treadmill, unfulfilled, I'm here to tell you not to lose hope. My goal with this chapter is to inspire you to be bold, bright and brave in the way in which you choose to make a living. Whether that is following a career path or just taking home that cheque, time is our greatest currency and you must invest yours wisely.

As a consequence of living through the health, economic and social upheavals of the pandemic, never before have terms like languish and burnout been trending quite as much. In fact, we are currently going through what is globally being referred to as 'The Great Resignation'. Many of us have taken a long hard look at our work-life balance and are deciding to be more intentional about the ways we spend and invest this time.

Let's get up close and personal with the subject of work, because you only get one lifetime and I want you to live yours to its absolute best. I want to explore the ways in which work and career inform our identities and take a closer look at our relationship with the broader economic system we call capitalism. Shall we get into it?

I was three months shy of my eighteenth birthday when I found out I had been accepted into the Paris Institute of Fashion to study fashion design. Upon graduating high school and completing a two-year course at TAFE in the same subject, I had made the decision that four years of uni was not to be my destiny, but I remained hungry for more education and also wanted to travel. So I came across a school in Paris that offered a summer course in fashion to international students. It seemed like a faraway dream, to move halfway across the world to live and study in the city I had been obsessed with since I was six: the birthplace of fashion, where only people like those I'd read in *Vogue* would visit.

I sent off my application and short of three months later I received my letter of acceptance. I still have it, in a shoebox in my closet. The tuition fee was the next hurdle. Nine thousand dollars. The largest sum of money I had ever comprehended in my life thus far, and frankly the two cafe jobs I worked wouldn't even begin to cover it. So, with my parents' hands in mine, I made my way to the bank and applied for a personal loan to cover the full amount.

Just like that, Deni was going to Paris. In the lead-up to my departure, my parents took me to Melbourne on a shopping trip to buy some essentials. At the top of our list was a good suitcase. Once we made our way to Melbourne, I told my parents I wanted to take them to the designer stores I had spent my whole teenage life reading about and soak in some inspiration for what was to be a fashion-filled summer ahead. We reached the corner of Collins and Russell streets in Melbourne, and the Louis Vuitton store beckoned, in all its glory, across the intersection. It had fast become one of my favourite labels.

As we entered the store, the lights glowing the most perfect amber hue, I talked my parents through the history of the house, its luggage origins and the humble beginnings of its namesake founder, Monsieur Louis Vuitton.

'You know a lot about our brand,' noted a sales assistant.

'I'm a fashion student,' I replied, beaming with pride.

'Deni's getting ready to go study in Paris,' my dad exclaimed, with even more pride than myself.

Upon inspecting the suitcases, I explained to my parents the house's iconic monogram logo designs.

'Deni, these suitcases are beautiful. Do you want me to buy you one?'

Bless my unknowing father. These suitcases cost more than his and Mum's combined weekly income.

'Tata, they're way too expensive. It's okay, we're just appreciating their beauty.'

His cheeks started to get red. 'Well, how much are they?'

When the sales assistant advised him of their four-figure price tag, I watched as my dad's head and shoulders dropped. He remained silent and as we made our way out onto Collins Street he began to cry quietly.

'Tata, what's wrong?' I asked.

He turned to me and told me he was upset that he couldn't afford to buy me this luggage from my favourite fashion designer for my special trip to Paris. I wrapped my arms around him and told him I didn't need fancy luggage and that, regardless, one day we would be able to afford it. Today was just not that day. We made our way to Myer instead, buying a more than adequate suitcase for a fraction of the cost.

I'll never forget how much my heart hurt watching him. A grown man, crying because his job did not allow him to buy this thing his son so desperately had longed for. My dad was crying as a result of the trappings of the capitalist world we lived in, which stacked the odds against working-class migrants like him. A world that told me, via advertising, that Louis Vuitton was the height of luxury, while I also knew from my own lived experience that this world wasn't one I belonged to. I didn't know all of this then, but I know it now.

The following week, I realised that perhaps a backpack might come in handy, and so I borrowed one from my cousin. A proper 'backpacking' backpack. Around the bag's front zipper, I wrapped a navy-blue Prada store ribbon. I don't remember how I acquired the ribbon, maybe someone I knew gave it to me, maybe it was from a fragrance purchase, I can't be sure. But hey fucking presto, I had a 'Prada' backpack to travel with. This silly little logo on a ribbon that surely cost less than a dollar to produce suddenly made me feel like I was part of the luxury world of fashion.

Have you ever felt simultaneously way out of your league but also as though you belong? That was the paradox I lived in when I attended fashion school in Paris. That feeling has never really gone away. It was there when I started interning at magazines like *Cosmo UK* and *British Vogue*. It was there when I got a job as an assistant stylist at the house of Burberry. It was there when I landed my fashion ed role at *Cosmo*, and it continues to rear its ugly head to this day, even now as I write this book. It's called 'impostor syndrome' and it's a feeling many of us will experience many times over.

What is impostor syndrome?

If you're unfamiliar with this term, to put it simply, impostor syndrome is the experience of feeling like a phoney. You feel as though at any moment you are going to be found out and those around you will realise that you do not, in fact, have the right or the privilege to occupy the space in which you live and work. Impostor syndrome is likely the result of multiple factors, including personality traits like perfectionism, as well as systemic causes like family, cultural and class background.

The first time I heard this term I couldn't escape it. It's become a global buzzword but isn't always clearly defined, so for that reason I think it merits a bit of a deeper exploration here.

Impostor syndrome is loosely defined as doubting your abilities and feeling like a fraud. It disproportionately affects high-achieving people, who find it difficult to accept their accomplishments. If we dig a little deeper within that category of person you'll find it ever-present in women as well as minority groups, including BIPOC and LGBTQIA+ people. If you belong to any of these groups, this will likely be no surprise to you. When you experience systemic oppression or are directly or indirectly told through cultural messaging that you don't deserve success, you will come up against impostor syndrome.

Perhaps you've been given a platform or a space that you never thought you'd occupy: a promotion, children, a partner; I mean, the list is as varied as it is long.

If this resonates with you, let's sit with that for a moment. And then let's start thinking about how we can start trying to combat impostor syndrome within ourselves.

Assess the facts

You are wherever it is you are for a reason. Have you stepped into a new phase of professional success? Found a partner you might not think you're truly worthy of? Honey, these things have been given to you because your actions have made them happen. So it's time to own your efforts.

Let go of the perfectionist

That snow queen knows what's up. It is your idealised concept of what the person in that space you currently occupy should look like that is holding you back from allowing yourself to occupy it. Let. It. Go.

Cultivate self-compassion

Compassion is such an underrated quality: the nice guy always gets a bad rap. I want you to direct that compassion you feel towards others back towards yourself. At the heart of impostor syndrome is a tendency towards self-criticism, so honey, let's switch that out for self-compassion.

Share your failures and your feelings

It is your 'failures' that are likely informing the way you currently feel, but you're not the only person who feels this way, so don't be afraid to be vulnerable with the people you trust. A negative feeling shared is a negative feeling halved, and I've found that, in sharing my own insecurities I've had around impostor syndrome, I've opened up space and 'given permission' for others to do the same.

Celebrate your successes

Take the time to properly celebrate YOU. Celebrate the moments, big and small, because life is too precious not to, and the more time you spend sitting in your impostor syndrome, the less you have to enjoy the moment. And please, for the love of God, stop talking things down. You didn't 'just' get a promotion. You didn't 'just' start your own business. You earned a promotion through your achievements; you've done the hard yards of starting a fucking business; so queen, now go get your crown.

My socioeconomic background has been at the root of almost all of my impostor syndrome. When my career trajectory pivoted to somewhat of a front-facing 'personality', for the longest time I would describe myself in media interviews as 'just the wog boy from Geelong, from a working-class family'. My business partner/manager/dear friend, Pru Corrigan, pulled me up on it one day, enquiring why I would always 'sell myself short' when the questions of my success came up. 'You are so much more than a working-class son of migrants,' she told me. 'You are also a hard-working human from a hard-working family who has earned their seat at the table. Be proud of that journey. Be proud of how far you've come.' Whenever I now default to framing my background in a modest, almost apologetic way, I stop myself and think of that conversation.

It can be hard to realise your own worth when so much of society's status calculator is based around job titles, annual salary, which school you went to, which suburb you grew up in and what the label is on the back of your shirt. As I write this, I'd like to also acknowledge my privilege. You might be reading this with a cultural background different to my own, from a community that is far more marginalised than mine is. I am an able-bodied, male-passing, light-skinned brown human, from a family that, while working class, had the privilege of working at all.

That might not be your lived experience. You may not have been afforded the privilege of even having a seat pulled up for you at the table. The privilege of walking into a bank and getting a loan to travel and study. Implicit bias and ableism and gender discrimination and ageism and queerphobia and systemic racism may have played very serious roles in your exclusion from the spaces I have had the privilege to work and therefore exist in. The world can be a challenging place to navigate at the best of times, less so if you are white, able-bodied, cisgender, heterosexual and male. Inequalities in hiring processes, salary gaps and between whole classes of people are very real.

Currently, Australia's national gender pay gap is 13.8 percent and, on average, women earn $256 less than men annually. With the rising costs of living, from petrol prices to the real estate market, $250 can mean the difference between eating and going without. It can be the difference between keeping the electricity on or having it turned off, or having money for essentials like sanitary items and healthcare. Statistics suggest that half of the Australian population has private health insurance, meaning that half of us do not. Fifty percent of Australian homes receive government welfare. While the current unemployment rate is sitting at a lower-than-average 4.2 percent, never before have the rates of partial employment and underemployment been so high. This is all not to mention the chronic, and worsening, issue of housing affordability in this country.

Where does one head when they feel as though there is nowhere left for them to go, due to broader structural factors coupled with the individual life choices we've made within the narrow framework that has been made available to us? One day my mother turned to me and said, 'I have no hope at a second chance of career, Deni. My time has passed.'

Oh, but it hasn't. I promise.

✦

Do you remember your first job? Your first pay cheque? How did it make you feel?

I'll never forget mine. I was fourteen and nine months, the minimum legal age required to work in Australia. I worked at a bakery/cafe, between two to three shifts a week and every single weekend without fail. I was on minimum wage and I loved every minute of it. Working for my own money made me feel accomplished; it made me feel mature and responsible and independent. My first pay cheque was $174. I still remember looking at my payslip and smiling from ear to ear. I earned that money. All by myself. And I wanted to see that number grow. I put myself down for extra shifts and suddenly I could feel my parents' work ethic running through my veins. Again: the apple and the tree.

This memory got me thinking about the reasons work has become such an integral part of our identities. I recently listened to a brilliant Ted Talk given by Sharon Belden Castonguay, an adult developmental psychologist with more than twenty years of career development experience. Sharon explains that through much of human history, people didn't have the luxury of choosing their 'line of work'. Humans simply did what their parents did, while others were prescribed jobs based on where they came from, their race, gender and social class. After two industrial revolutions, humans started to move away from their farms and into bigger cities, to work in factories and plants across the world. It's giving Homer Simpson energy.

Suddenly we – or, at least, those of us either born into the middle class or above, or who gain entry to these classes through a combination of luck, timing, education and/or hard work – were filled with choice. Even so, nowadays most people don't make career decisions rationally but rather based on deeply held, often unconscious biases that their parents passed on to them or they picked up on via the social environments they existed in. I'd hazard a guess that most of us have in some way or another been in jobs that didn't fill our cups because we felt as though there was no other option. Sound familiar?

Sharon continued by explaining that we tend to internalise the social biases we see around us and then typically follow the career paths of others, or we try to consciously follow an opposite path. When I think about my own work trajectory, it started very much in that vein. I watched as my parents worked multiple jobs for most of my upbringing. Following their stint in factories, Mum and Dad became commercial cleaners. At any given time their contracts would include cleaning supermarkets, office buildings, motels and department stores, my brother and I sometimes tagging along to help after school. In my experience, there is no experience quite as humbling as emptying someone else's rubbish bins or cleaning the toilets they've sat on.

We once worked in an office building in the city, in the taxation department. The well-dressed folk who remained inside when we began our shift treated us as though we were invisible. On the odd occasion that they looked up from their desk to lock eyes with me, their stare made me feel less than. It can really fuck with your sense of self-worth when you are made to feel as though you're at the bottom of the food chain.

I watched my parents grow their cleaning business tremendously, over ten years, to a place where they were taking in an annual turnover of a million dollars. They were, for want of a better term, 'killing it'. Until, almost overnight, their whole business shut down. They lost one of their biggest clients and went from employing cleaners to clean grocery stores to collecting trolleys themselves in the car park of our local shopping plaza. That change in income, lifestyle and ultimately self-worth was rapid and demoralising. My heart swelled with sadness for my parents. It was a stark reminder that at any given moment, no matter how hard you work, your whole life can change. Because, remember, everything is temporary.

Fast-forward to my own career as an adult, and I can see now, with the benefit of hindsight, the ways in which the fashion world rubbed off on me quicker than I realised. It was another steep learning curve in the impacts of your work environment, as I internalised the unconscious bias of my employers and colleagues. In the early years I often accepted without question that I would style celebrities for free, in exchange for 'Instagram mentions'. I later accepted a magazine salary at *Cosmo* not at all equivalent to my output of work, under the not so thinly veiled logic that 'a million girls would kill for that job'. (That's a *Devil Wears Prada* quote, if you don't know.)

My first encounter with interning was in London. I got my first foot in the door of the fashion industry one day a week at a public relations agency, via a work colleague's sister who needed interns for London Fashion Week. I worked for ten days straight, assisting the agency for the busiest week of their year, beginning most days at 7 am and ending after 9 pm. I loved every second of every minute of every hour of those ten days. The rush was intoxicating: the fashion, the people, the exposure to this world I had only ever dreamed of. I felt like Whitney Port, living my own *The City* fantasy.

When I was told that the internship didn't pay anything, I didn't even bat an eyelid. This is what I knew I had to do. I had a retail job to supplement my internship and parents back home who were a phone call and a Western Union transfer away. I was fortunate.

My three months of interning 'paid off', and following that gig I was given a job at another agency where I spent nine months working in PR. It was a job I loved. Not too dissimilar to my desire to be a lawyer, being a good publicist meant having the gift of the gab and, honey, I had it. But it was around this time that I decided I wanted to pursue a career in magazines and so, with my director's blessing, I jumped ship and went over to 'mag land'.

Interning in magazines, in London, was gruelling. I interned four days a week, sometimes five, and resorted to getting a night job in a call centre to make ends meet. My internship day began at 8 am and would end at around 5.30. I would then catch a train over to the other side of London to work in the call centre from 6.30 to 11.30 pm. Those working days were some of the longest, and yet I never once found it to be problematic.

My last internship in London was at *British Vogue*, the holy grail of magazine dreams; it would also be both my longest internship at six weeks, and the only one that paid me. I got fifty pounds a week to put towards transport and lunch. I ate a lot of sushi rolls in those weeks, alongside two-pound chicken burgers I'd buy on the high street closest to my flat. I vividly remember one desperate day, emptying out my wallet to pour eight pounds in coins on the mattress. I was waiting for my next pay cheque to come through and I refused to call my mother to ask for help, so I stretched those eight pounds out over a four-day period. I bought one-pound microwave meals from Poundland down the road and walked to and from work every day, which took me just under an hour each way. The things you do to save a buck, right?

Three years later, when I finally scored my job at *Cosmo* in Australia, I couldn't believe my luck. I had interned there for six whole months, one day a week, while working full time in retail. What I observed was that all the other interns in the fashion cupboard were children who came from money. In they'd stroll carrying the latest designer bag, simply there to pass their uni credits, and there I was, a twenty-seven-year-old 'working-class wog boy' wearing a t-shirt from Kmart, working my goddamn ass off.

My first salary at *Cosmo* was just shy of forty thousand dollars a year. Did I mention that Sydney is one of the most expensive cities to live in the world? A lot of Cup-a-Soups were made for lunch. But the feeling that has remained with me all this time about those early days at *Cosmo* and the five years following was the way that working there made me feel. I was the first person to enter the office between 7.30 and 8 am and typically the last person to leave at night. I worked weekends, not because I was told to or made to feel like I had to, but because I genuinely wanted to.

I had spent my whole adolescence reading magazines, *Cosmo* among them, and suddenly I had the privilege and honour to work at the world's highest-selling women's magazine. Honey, if there was Kool-Aid to be drinking, I was guzzling that shit by the gallon. I was so proud of that role, in love with the chosen family that was formed and genuinely honoured to be part of a team that sent out a product every month informing and empowering women (and humans of other genders) all over Australia.

But, suddenly, it was pulled from under me. The day the magazine closed and our whole team were made redundant was one of the most heartbreaking days of my life. It felt like it was both happening in slow motion and passing by in a blur. But there was a silver lining: I realised how much the label 'Deni from *Cosmo*' had become integral to my sense of who I was and where I stood in the world. The process of giving up that identity would turn out to be more painful, though ultimately rewarding, than the grief and financial fallout of the redundancy itself.

In Sharon's Ted Talk, she says that during the industrial revolution of the digital kind, it was largely preached that when passion dictates business decisions, you will 'never work a day in your life'. With some time and space away from *Cosmo*, I was able to stop and take stock of the state of my life, and many truths began to reveal themselves. I began to unpack who I was and what I wanted to be in a professional sense. I had become so invested in the *Cosmo* masthead that, with every issue that went to print, I took a step further away from what it was I wanted to do.

Around eighteen months after *Cosmo*'s closure, my dad said to me, 'Deni, you don't need *Cosmo*. You've got that phone in your hand. Make your own *Cosmo*.' His words rang in my mind all night.

I had developed a passion for storytelling from a very young age. I had developed a trained eye for curating content, and fashion was at the heart of who I was and the ways in which I share stories. Dad was right. It was at that moment I took to social media seriously and drafted up a business model and content schedule to turn 'Style by Deni', my Instagram account, from a personal scrapbook with sprinklings of styling to a full-time business.

I would provide a content offering that ranged from entertainment to lifestyle and fashion and beauty and sex and relationships and all the topics of conversation I missed having in the pages of the magazine. I could do this with my eyes closed. So I did. I would attract brands and clients that saw value in my voice and would want to work with me.

I would attract a manager who would see the worth in my vision and my voice; she would believe in my dreams and we would make them our great reality. That's a sentence I wrote, verbatim, and stuck on my vision wall. Six months later I would be introduced to Pru Corrigan, founder of One Daydream PR & Talent Management, and six weeks after she went on to become my business partner, mentor and member of my chosen family.

Sharon concludes her Ted Talk by saying that most people don't spend enough time figuring out who they are before making the decision of what they want to be. If we spend a third of our entire lives working for 'the man', chipping away for hours at a time just to bring home the bacon, how and when are we supposed to figure out who the fuck we really are? I watch my mum and dad continue to work their asses off, twelve hours a day, seven days a week. It's a superhuman effort, and yet some days their local cafe doesn't even make enough revenue to pay them a profit. It's fucking hard, and sometimes, much like love, all the hard work in the world is simply not enough.

This, dear reader, is where I would like to present to you an alternative mindset.

It goes without question that there are structural, material circumstances that factor into our career trajectory: gender, race and culture, socioeconomic status, religion, peer pressure, the individual attitudes of our parents to work and money. Not to mention the advertising and media we consume, and the way in which capitalism has slowly chipped away at our minds from the moment we got our first Happy Meal.

Within those constraints, it is ultimately up to you, and only you, to own your story. Even if you're among the percentage of humans who have no desire to pursue a career – honestly, mazel tov to you if so. Even if you're a primary caregiver to children, because let's remember that care work, no matter how chronically undervalued and underpaid or unpaid, is essential work. It's about realising which career choices serve you so that you can live authentically, according to your own desires around work and its place in your life. We are all of equal value, and in an economy that can see you go from the CEO to the cleaner in a hot damn second, we should all be treated as such.

The moral of this chapter is to say that if we are already spending a great chunk of our lives working, let's make it count. At the risk of sounding like I'm giving you a Ted Talk myself, I want to look over at you and exclaim, 'LOVE THIS FOR YOU'. Whatever 'this' looks like is entirely up to you. And you know what? That, my darling, is the best damn part.

We've arrived at the point where I'm going to ask you some big, broadbrush questions to get you started on a long self-reflection that will allow you to start living your career story on your terms. I want you to consider the following.

Over to you, darling

Upbringing

- How did your social environment growing up inform your relationship with work?
- Has your parents' work life informed yours?
- Did your parents encourage you to pursue your passions or pressure you to follow a career path prescribed by them?

Your current work

- Do you genuinely like what you do for a living?
- Does your job authentically reflect who you are as a person, and your values?
- Have you ever felt like there is 'no other option', or it is 'too late' to begin a career path that fulfils you?
- Does waking up and getting ready for work fill you with more levels of excitement or dread? Understanding, of course, that no single job can feel great *all* of the time.
- What would you say is the ratio between feeling fulfilled and unfulfilled?
- Are you fulfilled with the lifestyle your job currently affords you to live?
- Does your current job turn your internal light switch off or are you simply moving through the motions of the daily grind?
- Do you struggle to make ends meet, live beyond your means and feel overwhelmed by pressure to work to survive?

Your future path

- Have societal expectations of age and gender played into where you have landed professionally?
- What are your greatest passions and how do they, if at all, relate to your job?
- What is your understanding of capitalism, and can you place how it has informed your relationship with work?
- To be completely frank, what are some things you could do right now that would have future you thanking present you for the kick-ass work life you're going to have?
- Is there a course you can enrol in? A new skill you could learn or an old one you could reignite? Is there a way you can road-test your desired work path by looking for an internship, work experience, no matter what age you are?

And finally, the big questions that underpin all of this:

- Has who you are informed what you do?
- Would you like it to?

Please, carve out time to truly give some thought to all of this. Reflect on your answers with a knowing that whatever they are, you are in control of your life's trajectory. You can change vehicles and routes anytime you choose. Write that shit down; be intentional. Self-awareness is the MVP. Self-awareness arms us with the tools to resist internalising the many unconscious social biases that shove us into pigeonholes. Self-awareness also supports our future decision-making, allowing us to make decisions on our own terms, within a mental framework of our making.

It's time for one last exercise.

Over to you, darling

Step outside of yourself for a moment. I want you to dig deeper and identify the ways in which what you do for a living impacts your life and relationships, and reflects your identity. Are your job, career and professional life aligned with who you are at your most authentic?

Remember that vision board we made back in Chapter 3? And the words we pulled out to describe ourselves – the images and emotions and vibes we put together as a visual representation of our authentic expression?

If you're anywhere near your board, go and have a look at it. If it's on your phone, pull it up.

Does what you have on your vision board reflect what you do for work?

If the answer is no, that's okay. I'm sure you've heard of the terms 'work to live' and 'live to work'. Those terms are a bit like sexuality: they describe a spectrum of desire and behaviour, and all of us sit somewhere on that spectrum (and even then it varies for us between different life stages). If you are very much a work-to-liver, you just keep doing you and make sure you're happy doing so.

However, if you, like me, identify somewhere closer to the other side of the spectrum, as someone who is career-driven, then the follow-up question would be, would you like your authentic identity to be reflected in the work you do?

If you're a live-to-worker, I'd love you to come up with five keywords of how you would like your job to feel, or how you'd like it to make you feel. Write those words down and then think about what sort of job might generate those feelings within you. If you can't narrow down the job, think about the industries it could exist in more broadly or maybe it's more of a vibe. Do you want a job that involves travel, or creativity, or numbers, or sports, or film, or teaching, or the environment? Keep thinking – and then visualise.

Which images come to mind when you think of the work you can see yourself doing every day, the people you would work with and your desired work-life balance? Remember, we need to balance tangible and specific images with an aspirational vibe here.

Okay, now go to Google Images. Save. Screenshot. Print. Vision board. You know the drill now.

Surround yourself with those visual cues. Feel them. Believe them. Say them out loud. Remembering that you must still do the hard work to manifest these images in your life.

Right now I want you to dance. Let's press Play.

🕊 Dance break 🕊

'Work' – Rihanna feat. Drake
I want you to shake your ass to a woman who has become a trailblazer in so many ways as both an entrepreneur and inspiration, from the humblest of beginnings.

> **'Suddenly I See' – KT Tunstall**
> This song is from the opening credits of *The Devil Wears Prada*, one of my favourite movies of all time. On the first day of every fashion internship I've had, I listened to this song on my commute to the many publishing/media buildings I walked into. It's like a ray of sunshine to me. My hope is that it may bring you closer to a day where suddenly you too find yourself in the exact place you want to be.

Our very own Louis Vuitton

By the end of 2020 I'd spent my first year as a full-time content creator for my business 'Style by Deni' and my parents had finally started to find their feet as cafe owners. It was a beautiful moment where we could each celebrate the other's accomplishments.

Mum, Dad and I were in Melbourne. We were visiting my brother and sister-in-law, who had recently given birth to their daughter, my niece Sofia. We parked, as we always do, at Crown Casino.

Crown is also home to a handful of luxury stores. As we reached the ground floor of the building, I noticed my parents walking towards the stores rather than to the exit.

'Where are we going?' I asked.

'I just want to pop into some of the shops,' said my mother. 'We want to buy your brother and sister-in-law a present.'

I should have known that something was up when we made our way into Louis Vuitton. Mum asked around for diaper bags, and as we waited for the sales assistant to check their stock, Mum asked me if there were any bags I liked.

'Of course there are, doll, but I can't afford to buy any just yet,' I said.

I noticed Dad come closer. 'Yes, but we would like to buy you one.'

'What do you mean?' A lump formed in my throat.

'We're both so proud of everything you've achieved this year and we want to buy you something that reminds you of all your hard work and just how proud of you we are.'

The lump got more pronounced. 'But I don't need anything.'

My father said, 'Well, we never got to get you that bag when you went to Paris, so now we finally can.'

The three of us hugged and almost began to cry. I had spotted a bag when we walked in and pointed it out to my mum.

As the store assistant wrapped up the bag for me, I began to cry once again. I recounted to her the story of what had happened over a decade ago at their Collins Street store and she exclaimed that of the many humans who walk in and out of their store, she had never seen a more emotional and loving family purchase.

My dad finally got to have this moment of gifting me a symbolic piece of the world I'd fallen in love with as a child.

A short six months later, I wanted to repay them for this gesture, a token of my pride and gratitude for all of their support in me. I bought my dad a wallet and my mum a diary she had wanted for quite a few years. When I gave the gifts to them both in our living room, my dad cried. So did my mum.

I went to bed that night thinking about our work and career trajectories. The ways in which the capitalist system and the many structural layers of our own identities had informed our relationships with work and money. The way that these, in turn, informed our levels of self-worth and often lack thereof.

In these moments, these objects from a French luxury fashion label meant so much more than just pieces covered in logos. They represented hard work and determination. They represented the migrant journey my parents went on and the lives in which they had worked so hard to offer more opportunities to their children. They represented the work ethic which they instilled in me, and the gratitude I had for them for always supporting my passions.

Just like Jennifer Hudson in the *Sex and the City* movie, we now all had 'Our very own Louis Vuitton', and just as Carrie Bradshaw's assistant also felt, these luxury objects meant so much more than surface-level status-seeking. They represented hard work, accomplishment and aspiration – and that, my darlings, can feel pretty damn fabulous.

Affirmation

I am in control of my life's trajectory.

I listen with great care to my internal compass.

I am grateful for its direction.

*I can and will change its course when my spirit calls
   me to.*

*I am grateful for the abundance with which
   I am blessed.*

7.

Honouring your vessel

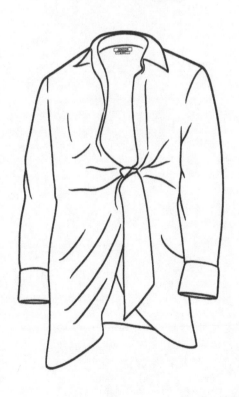

L et me invite you to the setting in which I'm writing this chapter. I'm in an Uber, though I'm sure I won't be here by the time we've worked our way to the end. I am wearing an oversized pink t-shirt by Balenciaga that has the word GAY emblazoned across the chest. As we speak, the state of Florida is looking to sign off on its 'Don't Say Gay' bill and my heart feels heavy. I feel bloated today, and the shapelessness of this shirt helps to hide that and is the kind of armour I need.

Before we jump in, it's worth noting this chapter will touch on my own disordered eating, and eating disorders more broadly. If this is triggering content for you, I respect your decision to pass it, but if you do choose to stick with me and work our way to healing, together, I'll leave some helpful support resources at the end.

As I write this, I am the heaviest I have ever been. I seldom weigh myself. I've done it on and off over the years and, as an all or nothing kinda human, my relationship with the scales went from one that consisted of weekly weigh-ins to times like now, when I typically avoid the scales unless for a very specific kind of self-sabotage. Last night was one such night.

I thought I'd give myself a little writing break and start the hunt for an outfit (read: multiple outfits) for my upcoming birthday party, because I love nothing more than a costume change. When I turned thirty, I declared that every year should be worthy of a celebration because life, my friends, is too short not to celebrate. Every birthday party I've had since has come with a theme and a dress code.

Do you enjoy a themed party? I fucking froth a theme, I always have. There is something so incredibly liberating about stepping into a different kind of persona. I find it fascinating that humans don't often give themselves permission to truly express themselves unless they're in costume. You can tell a lot about a person based on the 'costume' they wear. It's almost like being ourselves is not permission enough to shine.

I spend most of my life these days wearing whatever I want to, no matter the occasion or time of day even. If I want to wear a ball gown to the supermarket, you'd better believe I will. Everyone who follows me on the 'gram will understand how truly, madly, deeply I love clothes, and how much this love is an integral part of who I am. So it would make a lot of sense then that the biggest discomfort I have around my body is when it serves as an obstacle between myself and fashion. When I am naked in the shower or making love to my partner Archie, I never once feel uncomfortable or even remotely disgusted by my body and weight. But when it comes to fashion – well, that little bitch knows exactly how to make me feel like absolute shit.

Last night I was scrolling through a selection of some of my favourite online stores when I stumbled across what could be a perfect party outfit. This year's party theme was Studio 54, and the muses I wanted to channel most were Bianca Jagger and Grace Jones. My Bianca look would be an easy one to put together, but it was my Grace Jones that I needed to perfect. She is, after all, a Queer icon.

During my search I came across the most epic bodysuit, the kind of look that makes my heart skip a beat. It was neon lime, skin-tight and a mixture of transparent nude-illusion mesh and lime stripes across the body. It was a design by Mugler, one of my favourite fashion houses, and has been worn in black by Miley Cyrus. It was the definition of a fashion moment. A little more expensive than I would like, but it was my birthday and so the justification for its price tag slowly marinated in my mind as I looked at picture after picture of the model wearing it. I looked at the size run and was surprised to discover that it did in fact cater for up to my size, and over in fact – bravo, Mugler.

For context, I wear anywhere between a women's size fourteen (Australian) to a size sixteen, depending on the fit and cut of the garment. It's also worth noting that I am the size of the 'standard' Australian woman. I have only recently come around to wearing more fitted fashion pieces, after having worn almost exclusively oversized silhouettes for a time. Even so, a skin-tight bodysuit is quite the brave choice for any human, and while it's not by any means outside of the wheelhouse of my aesthetic, it's a commitment. As I looked upon the fit model, thoughts immediately began to race through my mind:

Well, it's not going to look like that on you, Deni. If you were skinny, it would.

Everything looks good on skinny people. If I were skinny, I could wear anything.

Maybe I could try it and just commit to losing five kilos before the party. Could I actually do that, though?

I'll have to buy both the fourteen and sixteen and see which fits. How annoying. If I were her size, I wouldn't have to do that.

How am I in the worst shape of my life? How did I let myself get here?

The thoughts came in thick and fast, and in a bid to either confirm or deny my intrusive thoughts I walked over to my mum's bathroom, where the scales were, and weighed myself. As I looked down at the number, it confirmed what I already knew to be true. This was the most I had weighed in my thirty-four years.

I got off those scales and proceeded to be upset for the rest of the night. Then I did what I always do when I feel this way. I ate. I ate an ice cream with my mum. Knowing full well its calorie count.

This is all to say that my relationship with my body, and the ways in which this impacts my self-worth, is a complicated one.

How is yours? Shall we get into it? Do you need to make yourself a cuppa before we do? Please feel free to. I've got my takeaway double-shot mocha in hand and I'm just chilling in the Uber, so honey, you do you and I'll be right here waiting for you when you get back.

We live in a world obsessed with body image. That's just a straight-up fact. In a society that continually changes its beauty standards, it can be difficult to remain positive about oneself.

Over my twelve years of working primarily in women's media, I have seen the rhetoric of what is 'hot' and what is 'not' change drastically over the years. Skinny was in and then skinny was out; then curves were in but you couldn't be fat, until one day terms like 'fat positivity' entered the zeitgeist and brands like Victoria's Secret were effectively cancelled for their long history of perpetuating unrealistic beauty standards. While women are told to chase the perpetual fountain of youth and different forms of the ideal body, terms like #Daddy and 'Dad Bods' trend the world over, giving men some more freedom in self-image – unless of course you're Jonah Hill and the internet collectively ridicules your waistline.

Society implicitly endorses the very public scrutiny and judgement of women's bodies. The same photograph of a Hollywood starlet can lead to her being described variously as anything from gaunt to svelte, voluptuous to overweight, depending on the media outlet. The mere sight of anything that resembles a baby bump sends tabloid culture into overdrive. Adele and Rebel Wilson are simultaneously crucified and celebrated for losing weight, and Oprah Winfrey's waistline has been a decades-long topic she has frequently discussed on her talk show.

At any given time humans are told they're too fat, too thin, too old, too young, young and hot, not old enough, not 'old and hot' enough. Drop a dress size, book that Botox appointment, try this new diet, take this new supplement, Facetune your photos, sign up to F45, exercise five times a day, wake up at 5 am but also remember #balance and #youveearnedit, as if food is something we must earn in order to consume. The list is as long and ever-changing as it is exhausting.

We have become so obsessed with what we put into our mouths that the diet industry is one of the most profitable in our country and it is growing at a rapid rate. According to ibisworld.com, the market size, measured by revenue, of the weight-loss services industry is $477 million in 2022. This figure is expected to increase by 4.4 percent this year alone.

All the while, body image struggles are robbing you of real-life experience. As a child, I remember some of my cousins would avoid family functions because they were too self-conscious about their weight and could drop a size in time to 'fit into that dress'. As if wearing something in their size was simply not an option.

I've watched family, friends and former partners forgo swimming in the summer because of their anxiety around getting into bathers. I've seen girlfriends, in droves, take themselves off the 'dating market' solely because of their body and size, lacking the self-worth to feel as though another would find them even remotely desirable. I've had sex with the lights off because of body dysmorphia and the fear that a bed partner would be revolted by my midsection.

Did you know that 96 percent of women are unhappy with and/or would like to change their physical appearance? In Australia approximately one million humans each year suffer from an eating disorder, with women significantly more likely to experience this. The increasing trend in young people's levels of concern about their body image was reported by the Butterfly Foundation to have peaked at 31 percent just before the pandemic hit in 2020, up from 26 percent in 2015. This year-on-year data highlights the need for body image to be seen as a national mental health concern.

What is at the root of this self-worth crisis?

In every conversation I've had with Elise about the various pillars of our identity, she steers me back to our environment, to our childhood and the way said pillars were formed in our minds, largely by way of our parents, our culture and the social structures we both observed and grew up in. If we dig a little deeper we will find that historically, different cultures will have very differing beauty norms and ways in which they celebrate beauty.

In Tonga, beauty is marked by large physical size. In Kuwait, where women exercising is a taboo, wives are frequently prized as decorative items to fill up the house: the bigger, the more opulent. In Fiji, girth has long been revered in a woman as a sign of health, wealth and fertility. The island of Tahiti has been home to a practice called ha'apori, literally meaning 'to fatten': young women were plumped and presented to the chief for beauty and fertility inspection. With these global variations in mind, it becomes apparent that thinness as a dominant representation of beauty standards is a very Eurocentric, white, Western concept.

Growing up as a brown child in regional Victoria, I was surrounded by fuller-figured women and men who cherish nothing more than a hearty family meal. Food had always been at the centre of every celebration, and yet, in the mid-nineties something shifted. All the women in my family began yo-yo dieting. Jenny Craig and Weight Watchers were the weight-loss trends du jour and programs like Danoz Direct pumped out little electrode machines that you hooked up to your tummy to zap the fat and firm up the core. My mum bought many variations of these contraptions and even offered them up for me to try.

My brother never needed them: he was born with the athletic genes that the men on my mother's side of the family were 'genetically blessed' with. I, on the other hand, inherited the body shape of my father's side of the family: round in the face and at the waist. My dad's weight has fluctuated since he was a child, and I remember when I was about twelve myself watching Dad undergo a massive body transformation. Over the course of a winter, he would wake up early to run laps around our block, do star jumps in our living room and live solely on a diet of fish and rice. He dropped somewhere around thirty to thirty-five kilos.

What I will never forget were people's reactions. Family, friends and even members of our church celebrated Dad's transformation, sending the implicit message that he looked better now than he had before when he was larger. My observations of this before/after narrative were imprinted on my young, impressionable mind.

On the female side of the spectrum, I watched my mother try every fad diet under the sun. The cabbage soup diet; the Beyoncé 'Dreamgirls' diet, which called for drinking a blend of lemon juice and cayenne pepper. Mum even tried supplements and weight-loss pills.

I've watched aunties have their stomachs stapled, undergo lap band and gastric bypass surgeries. I went along, as a young child after school, to my mum's Jenny Craig and Weight Watchers meetings. Imagine sitting in a room with a group of mostly women, all of whom were made to stand on a scale and weigh themselves in a group environment. As part of this ritual, the drop of a kilo would be celebrated and the absence of any weight loss met with a 'There's always next week'.

Who told my mother she was overweight to begin with? It certainly wasn't my dad. My mum said that while, like everybody else, a constant display of models and celebrities in the media informed her own internal beauty standards, her insecurities have usually centred more on clothes. (Cue my obligatory 'apple, tree' comment here.) Mum told me, 'Whenever we would go shopping for an event like a wedding, I would hate not being able to fit into a dress straight off the rack. Fitting rooms made me feel insecure instead of empowered, and it was always fashion that drove me to dieting.'

Fashion was once again the perpetrator of this internal abuse. I have worked within the industry for well over a decade, and my eyes have consumed fashion imagery for even longer. I grew up in the era of the nineties supermodel: women like Naomi, Cindy, Linda and Kate stormed the runways of Versace and Mugler, and I noted how the fabric hung from their slender frames. In my late teens the world of pop culture made its way out of 'heroin chic' – an actual term used to describe a desirable aesthetic – and into the 'size zero' era. Starlets like Mischa Barton, Lindsay Lohan and Nicole Richie reigned supreme, and the woman behind their famous looks was Rachel Zoe.

If you're unfamiliar with Rachel, she played a pivotal role during the noughties to establish the image of the 'Hollywood stylist'. Her clients ranged from A-listers like Jennifer Garner, Anne Hathaway and Kate Hudson to the young hot things who were stumbling out of cars on their way to the Chateau Marmont, Chloe 'Paddington' bags in the nooks of their arms, sans underwear. At the height of her career, Rachel was rumoured to be handing out diet pills to her clients in a bid to keep them sample size. While she vehemently denied those rumours, there is a connection to be made between her influence on fashion and the perpetuation of some problematic beauty standards.

It was around the same time that Victoria's Secret fashion shows reached their all-time peak ratings. Each show featured the hottest pop singer of the time performing while thin models took to the runway in lingerie and angel wings. Think about the messaging behind that imagery for a moment: in order to 'get your wings' and fly, you had to be as tiny as those models were.

As a young Queer human obsessed with all things celebrity, I was soon influenced by these women to be as thin as humanly possible. It was around the age of eighteen that I became severely underweight. I had also just moved to Paris and it was the first time in my life that I could control the food I was consuming. All those years of living at home meant I became used to breakfast, lunch and dinner, all of which generally included meat and bread and always room for a late-night snack, typically ice cream. In Paris I could eat whatever I wanted, and in a bid to achieve the protruding collarbone aesthetic of that era, I restricted myself to eating one fruit cup, twice a day. I made excuses that it was to save more money to shop, but really I knew it was because I wanted to be a size zero. Nicole Richie was a size zero and I wanted that waif look as much as the girls in my fashion class did.

Upon my return from Paris my parents took one look at me and in a state of shock declared that I needed to be fed. 'You need to fatten up, Deni, what have you been eating over there?' So I returned to my mother's kitchen and slowly got back to a healthy weight.

Until one afternoon, at my grandparents' house, when someone made a comment that I had become chubby. I remember clear as day a relative pulling at my cheeks and tapping on my belly, as if to suggest the weight there was a new development. I reverted to controlling what I ate almost immediately. I was working at a denim store at the time and ate little more than a Boost juice and a sushi roll most days. My manager, who was also my cousin, sat me down one day to have a chat with me: 'Deni, I know what you're doing because I used to do it too. You need to eat solid meals, because this is a slippery slope and it won't end well.'

The mixed messages were overwhelming: one minute I'm too thin, the next I am chubby, and then once again too thin. I started weighing myself almost daily. Whenever the number went down, my self-esteem went up.

Looking back, I can see that the common thread was that whenever I was living alone, I could control what I ate, and no matter how out of control my life felt, the one thing I could control was what I put in my mouth. In London, following my breakup with Ben, I dropped to the lightest I had ever been. Photos of myself at that time show my collarbones protruding, and little to no fat hanging from my emaciated frame. With every Facebook photo album I posted came an onslaught of texts from family and friends back home saying: 'Deni, you're getting too skinny over there. Eat something please.' And yet, with every one of those comments, my internal dialogue felt affirmed, because I was finally skinny again.

It's no coincidence that around this time I was finding my feet in the fashion industry. In my roles at *British Vogue*, assisting one of London's top stylists and as a styling assistant at Burberry, every model I worked with became thinner and younger with every shoot. It wasn't uncommon to be shooting a fifteen-year-old girl for a fashion editorial that was targeted to women in their twenties and thirties. This beauty standard was unachievable to most: we were shooting teenagers, for fuck's sake, and yet no one seemed to care.

On one specific shoot for which we had a group of six female models, there was a smell of sick in the air as I buttoned up their Chanel dresses. Towards the end of the day, one of the models nearly fainted, and the photographer said, 'Someone fetch her a gummy bear, she needs sugar.' What she needed was more than a gummy bear, and yet at that moment it was a completely acceptable solution to a global problem plaguing our industry.

In January 2012, the fashion industry began slowly waking up to this skinny epidemic. Anna Wintour, editor of *American Vogue* and board member of the Council of Fashion Designers of America, issued a statement that went out to every designer in the country declaring that any photoshoot or fashion show must have food catered on set. The letter went viral the world over, and the industry finally started to own up to a long-overdue conversation about beauty standards, size expectations and eating disorders. Only that the issue extended beyond the industry – it informed the minds of so many observers consuming fashion content daily.

As if navigating the problematic beauty standards perpetuated by traditional forms of media wasn't enough, before long we also had Instagram to contend with: a photo-sharing app that would allow you to visually document your life to an online community. The 'influencer' was born. What could possibly go wrong? Spoiler alert: everything.

It might sound ironic of me to talk about the harmful effects of Instagram given that the app is in many ways my primary source of income, but it wasn't always this way. In the early days of social media, I threw myself into this world of image creation to fill my creativity-starved cup. I was working multiple retail jobs and trying as hard as I could to get my break in print media. Instagram offered up something that no magazine could: a democratic media-scape filled with endless opportunities and little to no application required. But what began as a cute way to share your life, from the latte you just ordered to the holiday you last went on, soon made way for bikini bodies, muscle enthusiasts and the hashtags #thighgap and #fitspo.

It's become common knowledge that social media isn't great for our relationships with our bodies, nor for our mental health. Multiple studies have found a strong link between heavy social media use and an increased risk of depression, anxiety, loneliness, self-harm and suicidal thoughts. Social media all too often promotes problematic beauty standards and leads to many of us experiencing feelings of inadequacy about our lives or appearance, likely both at the same time.

Once upon a time it was merely celebrities who we compared ourselves to, but now it's that fitness model you follow in Byron Bay or that personal trainer who's trying to sell you a membership to his new and improved bootcamp program. It's your neighbour or the woman you see at the school drop-off or that guy you met at the Beresford last Sunday. The fact that Photoshop and filters are readily available to users further plays into the perpetuation of unrealistic body image standards. Photoshop was once reserved for A-listers on magazine covers, but now anyone within arm's reach of Facetune and a YouTube tutorial can alter the way they look to unrecognisable proportions.

The worst part is that we have all at some point succumbed to the pressures of this narrative. So how the fuck is any one human supposed to have a healthy relationship with their body while navigating the wild world of socials?

My difficulties with body image reached an all-time peak while I was living in Sydney as I entered the city's robust and notoriously body dysmorphic gay scene. If you ever want to feel unhappy with your body, move to Sydney. Jokes aside, there is something about the combination of it always being so warm and the general air of body-obsessed humans that results in some of the most ripped bodies you will ever see. The potential for public scrutiny of your body increases if you're a gay man.

I got to know the figure of the 'muscle gay' well when I lived in Potts Point. I would watch them make their way out of Fitness First Kings Cross and then downstairs to Coles to buy their salmon fillets and spinach for dinner, while I headed straight to the ice cream section. I wanted to be like them. I longed to be like them. I also wanted to date them.

Nine months later I was dating a muscle gay, and it was at once thrilling and terrifying. My partner at the time had muscles in places I didn't know could exist. Whenever his shirt came off, it took all of my willpower to not audibly gasp. 'How the fuck does anyone achieve a body like that?' I asked him. He chalked it up to a combination of genetics, diet and exercise. Exercise he did, five days a week, seldom missing a morning.

Before long, I jumped on the bandwagon. I joined F45. I tried intermittent fasting, I drank protein shakes, which taste like shit and make you really gassy. At prime times on the gay calendar, I redoubled my efforts. Two workouts a day, more fasting, more shakes and sometimes a quick workout on a Saturday. I starved myself in the lead-up to Mardi Gras every year, and for what? To flaunt the sixpacks I had for so long dreamed of.

It didn't take long for my body to get to a very similar physique to my partner's. On one occasion he noticed that my biceps had become even bigger than his. It made me feel good. It made me feel strong and sexy, like a real man, the man the gay world so desperately wanted me to be.

Everyone back home noticed my body transformation with great acclaim. 'Look at those guns.' 'You're so ripped, man.' 'You're in the best shape of your life.' They were right, I knew I was, and hearing them say it further fuelled my desire to 'improve' my body. The irony of it all was that while I had never looked 'better' or more 'fit', my lifestyle choices couldn't have been worse for my health. I was partying every weekend, taking more party drugs than a human should have, and controlling what I did and didn't eat. I was also regularly consuming problematic fashion magazine rhetoric that continued to perpetuate the #fitspo movement.

But after a long, tried and tested formula of problematic coverlines at *Cosmo*, the tide started to shift. Let's talk about those coverlines for a moment: these are the words you see on the cover of a magazine. 'Get Fit Fast', '69 Ways to Have Better Sex', 'Bikini Ready', etc.; you get the vibe. A quick Google search reminded me of just how troubling some of the messaging in women's media was at the time I worked in the thick of it.

'Look Better Naked' was a coverline we ran alongside Kim Kardashian, the woman at the centre of a family that was changing beauty and body norms world over. First for good, and later – well, the jury's still out on just how positive the Kardashians' messaging has become. Other coverlines included 'Fast Track to FIT AF!' The express workout you'll want to try. Another boasted, 'All the Inspo for a Hotter, Healthier Bod'. Was 'hotter' really healthier, though? Other coverlines focused firmly on our faces. 'How to Fix Your Face After an Ugly Cry' is one I can't believe we actually ran. But we did, and Miranda Kerr graced said cover. It became one of our highest-selling issues that year.

It wasn't hard to connect the dots. We were part of an industry that's responsible for the beauty standards informing humans all over the country. Whether they were physically buying that month's issue of *Cosmo* or simply peeping at the cover on the newsstand, the messages were loud and clear.

Then a game-changing cover was released by our British sister, *Cosmopolitan UK*, starring Tess Holliday, the thirty-three-year-old model who made a career by being open about her struggle with weight and body positivity. The cover was slammed by British tabloids and, most notably, Piers fucking Morgan.

Our editorial team stated that, while the cover was a brave choice, it would be too risky to run in Australia. Sure, it was inspiring, but was it aspirational? There were so many assumptions that weighed down that term 'aspirational'. For decades, image-makers in the media like us had brought our own preconceptions to what women aspire to be. Evidently it was somehow aspirational of us to tell them their cry faces were ugly, but god forbid we should reflect a more representative range of their bodies on the cover of our magazine.

Shortly after *Cosmo* folded and I moved back home to Geelong, three major things happened.

First, I was living with Mum and Dad again, eating regularly, still moving my body and exercising when I felt like it. But I was also in close proximity to their cooking and the cafe they own. Before long my once 'gym-fit' body made way for what I felt was a healthier body shape. Over the course of the next eighteen months I would jump two dress sizes, from a ten to a solid fourteen.

The next two sliding-doors moments, which you've heard about already, happened in unison: we went into lockdown and I came out as non-binary. Against this backdrop entered a new app that would in some ways temporarily even the playing field of social media. TikTok was less filtered and more reactionary, and suddenly I had an app in my hands where people looked more like me. Trans and gender-diverse people, people of colour, people of all body shapes filled my 'For You' page with their strong voices and critical hot takes on the many racist and patriarchal systems that have shackled society for so long.

During the 2020 lockdown we also faced a global reckoning about race, fuelled by the Black Lives Matter movement. This reckoning filtered into the corporate world, and soon brands and organisations were left, right and centre finally being called out for the toxic narratives they had been perpetuating. In the firing line were magazines like *Vogue*, fashion institutions like Victoria's Secret and the once aspirational fitness and bikini influencers.

When the world is locked down and you can't visit the beach to post a selfie, people begin to realise that maybe these media depictions were more harmful than we initially realised. Khloé Kardashian was blasted for altering her body in the images she shared to her two hundred and thirty million followers. People were analysing procedures like BBLs (a Brazilian butt lift, which promises to make your backside look like a Kardashian's). Without access to their local injector, people started wondering whether Botox was something their 'ugly cry face' really needed.

With this renewed sense of perspective came a collective realisation that starving yourself to fit into a dress for a special event is a toxic exercise. The more fat-positive content I consumed, the quicker I realised that I didn't have to succumb to the size-zero mindset I had spent half my life trying to achieve.

During this season of rebirth, I started to set boundaries with my social media, something I had never done before. Anyone who made me feel bad about my own body was unfollowed. Seeing image after image of thigh gaps and washboard abs was only making me feel worse, and had triggered my disordered eating. The very term 'disordered eating' was only brought to my attention during lockdown. Suddenly I had a term that I identified with and which summed up my body journey in a nutshell. I never lived with anorexia or bulimia per se, but I knew that what I was doing was borderline eating disorder.

With so many brave humans taking to their proverbial microphones to share their body journeys, I finally knew where I sat on that scale and it gave me great power in staring my body-image demons straight in the eye. I, like I'm sure many of you did, put on a bunch of weight across 2020 and into 2021. When there is little to do and no places other than Coles to go, 'working for your summer body' seems like an unnecessary goal. People took up yoga and Pilates and meditation and exercise that feeds your soul rather than encouraging weight loss. I tried my hand at a few of these practices but only really stuck with meditating, the least physical exercise of them all.

Without even realising it, I put on more weight and now am between a size fourteen and sixteen. When I came out as non-binary, I was asked by many of my relatives if I wanted to 'turn into a girl', prompting yet another level of re-evaluation of my body. I knew that I had no desire to change any part of my genitalia or body, but it took a lot of time with myself to critically enquire within.

With all of these ups and downs in my relationship with my body has come a sharpened awareness of the following:

We are works in progress. Body acceptance, alongside self-love, doesn't involve arriving at a single destination. It's an evolution that will ebb as much as it will flow, and learning to accept that is where you'll find the power.

So, over the course of a few weeks and some very long baths, I began by sitting with myself, naked. I caressed my chubby cheeks, as if to say, 'It's okay, darlin', I love you.' I did the same to my belly and to all parts of my body that had felt heavier than they did before.

I looked at myself in the mirror and said out loud, 'I. Love. You.' I thanked my body for the journey we've been on. I began referring to my body as a vessel. A vessel that carries me through this life, bearing scars and trauma and resilience and strength. I apologised to it for all the times I had criticised its size, its number on a scale, or its digits reflected on the back of the waistband on my jeans.

How dare I be so cruel to it for all these years. How dare I continue to. Because remember, we're all works in progress.

Have you ever told your body that you love it – that you are proud of it? Have you acknowledged your body as a vessel that has carried you through every season of your life? That, my dear, is where I want you to start.

Let's do an exercise together. I want you to get naked. You can do this in your own time, when you're alone and feel safe enough to do so. When the time and place are right, remove your clothes and then let's do this, you and me (I say this in the least creepy way possible). I'd love for us to ideally be close to a mirror so that we can see our own beauty. If a mirror isn't handy, sitting alone – or standing – will be just fine.

I'll go first. We're all in this together, right?

Okay, give me a minute.

I'm back. How'd you go? Let me tell you, writing this book has been like stripping myself naked to all of you. I never imagined I'd be sitting here, actually naked, but I think it's necessary. Good thing I'm back at home and no longer in that Uber, otherwise this could've become awkward.

I always had this rule as a stylist that I would never ask my models to do something I wouldn't do myself. So, on more than one occasion, I would support them as such. Once I jumped into a freezing cold pool in my undies, during winter, to support the model I had cast to shoot our swimwear issue. Another time I had asked a celebrity to ride a horse, in the ocean, for a cover shoot. I had no idea she was terrified of the animal and had never sat on one before, so I got up on that horse and tested it for her first.

Empathy is a value I live by, and I can't possibly ask you to do this without first doing it myself, so let's go.

I want us to start with three deep breaths, in through the nose and out through the mouth. Ready?

First breath.

Second breath.

Third breath.

Okay, now with me, I want you to place your hands on your stomach as if you were to hug it, and repeat after me.

I thank you today, my beautiful vessel, for the strength with which you have carried me through this life.

I'm sorry if I've ever made you feel unworthy, not beautiful, too big, not big enough and everything else in between. I am sorry and I love you.

You are strong, you are beautiful, you are resilient, and you are worthy.

I love you and I will honour you for the rest of our journey.

I want you to do the same up at your chest, resting your palms on each arm.

Thank you, dear vessel, for the strength with which you have carried me.

I will love and honour you for the rest of our journey.

Now I'll ask you to look at yourself in the mirror. If you don't have one around, pull out your camera phone. Change it to selfie mode and get ready to talk. You might even want to film this so that you can save it as a reminder.

Repeat after me.

My darling [insert your name here],

Thank you for guiding me through this world, with your strength, your resilience and your beauty.

I am so tremendously proud of you.

I am sorry if I've ever made you feel as though you are not pretty enough, not worthy enough, not perfect enough. You are a marvellous creation and every highlight and flaw is perfect because you are a divine energy that is made with love.

You are beautiful.

You are worthy.

You are strong.

I love you.

Now give yourself a moment to come back into the room and over to this page.

I'll wait for you.

It can be hard to say such wonderfully power-filled affirmations to ourselves, and yet we do this every day to other people, giving compliments to friends, family and strangers.

The purpose of this exercise is to remind you that your body is an experience and it's a vessel; it's not just an image. It's time to reframe that mindset and honour the experience. Life is for living, and while the journey won't be linear, my hope is that you might use this exercise as a tool to remind yourself of your true worth. A tool to edge you closer to loving the vessel you are in. Let yourself feel the love you give so freely to others; give yourself compassion; think of the things you love about who you are and be your own damn hype girl. In doing so, we have the power to turn the lowest of body feelings into strength.

Before we close out this chapter, here are some things I'd like you to consider.

 Over to you, darling

- How have your environment, culture and family dynamic informed your relationship with your body and self-worth?
- Are you comparing yourself constantly to the images you see in the world? What can you do to change the narrative so that you're setting boundaries and consuming imagery that empowers you rather than fostering self-loathing?
- A solution to this I'd encourage you to try is to unfollow anyone who makes you feel bad about your body. I mean it. Removing harmful body standards from my newsfeed and replacing them with accounts that empowered me and liberated my relationship with my vessel was a game changer. Never underestimate the

power the images we consume daily has over us. I'll share some of my favourite body-positive accounts at the end of this chapter for you.

- What are some daily practices you can do that will strengthen your relationship with your vessel? If movement is your thing, could you give dancing, yoga or Pilates a try? It's worth turning to intentional forms of exercise that are focused on connecting to one's spirit rather than dropping numbers on a scale. Or it could be as simple as pouring yourself a bath and lathering your vessel with luxurious oils, honouring its form as you go, connecting with it sensually, in a way you might with a romantic partner.

If you're reading this and have little humans in your life, I'd love you to consider the following:

- Language is so incredibly important. Do you use language around children that is body positive rather than body negative?
- Can you diversify the media that children are consuming so as to encourage self-acceptance rather than continue to inform their minds with toxic unrealistic beauty standards?
- Ultimately, are you equipping them with conversations and tools to encourage empowerment and self-love?

I think it's time for us to wrap up with two of my favourite self-empowering songs for our end-of-chapter dance break.

🦢 Dance break 🦢

Let's begin with a song that puts a lump in my throat every time I listen to it. The lyrics and accompanying music video shine a light on our constant quest for perfection. It's a disease that so many of us struggle with, and it is only with a self-awareness of both it and the impacts of what we've been exposed to that we can walk towards a healthier relationship with ourselves. Press Play on:

'Pretty Hurts' – Beyoncé

Now let's turn to a song I listen to whenever I'm feeling down on myself. I want you to sing it loud, sing it proud, and remember that you are, in this moment, fucking perfect. It's time to change the voices in your head and start being kind to yourself. Let's listen to:

'Fuckin' Perfect' – Pink

Did that leave you feeling as empowered as it did me? I hope so. This chapter was a deep one, so thank you for coming here with an open heart; I feel so privileged that we get to be vulnerable together.

Fuck the skinny pile

I had recently come out as non-binary and I had never bought myself a dress. So one night in lockdown, I asked myself, 'What would I be if I were a dress?' I knew that I always felt good in a sharp silhouette, and that collars always made me feel confident, but I also knew I wanted the dress to be sexy. A blend of masc and femme. I looked towards one of my style icons and typed 'Kim Kardashian dress' into Google.

There it was, in all its glory: a white shirt dress by the new designer of the moment Jacquemus. Strong in its silhouette on the top half, a collared white shirt essentially, which cascaded down the model's chest like a scooped body of water, finishing around the waist with a tie that ruched into a miniskirt. If I were a dress, this is what I would be.

I jumped online and found the last one available in my size. It was on sale, and I couldn't have hit 'add to cart' sooner. A week later it arrived and when I tell you I squealed when I opened it, I mean it. Literal squeals of joy.

The dress was beautiful, chic and strong, just as I had wanted it to be. Until I slipped it on. I guess I had read the French sizing wrong; it was easily half a size too small for me. Even so, I somehow managed to button it up close. It was tight, but it fit. My internal dialogue kicked in: 'That's okay, we only have a few weeks of lockdown left, I'll just drop some weight between then and wear spanx if I need to underneath to smooth me out.'

Except I never lost the weight. I gained another five kilos, and then another two, and then suddenly I couldn't do up even one single button at the skirt level of the dress. Frustrated and filled with self-loathing, I hung it back up and exclaimed that I would leave it visible on my rack in a bid to inspire me to get into shape so that 'one day' I could eventually wear it.

And so, the 'skinny pile' was born. You know the pile. We all have one. A pile of clothes, some new, some old, all left unworn because we tell ourselves we will fit into them once more. We taunt ourselves with the notion that the weight we are now is not good enough and that we must get from this, to that, quick smart.

Over the course of the first few months of our short-lived post-lockdown freedom, I tried the dress on, knowing full well it wouldn't fit me. I thought that perhaps shaming myself into the fact that it didn't fit would inspire me to do something about it.

Except that it didn't, and it continued not to, for another six months. Every day I would look at that dress on the free-standing rack in my workspace and a twinge of anger would alert my insides that I was overweight. What's worse was that during that time my new-found genderfluid lease on life saw me online-shop more than ever, and I developed a habit of adding things to my 'skinny pile'. Pieces that arrived but didn't fit quite right or didn't sit as I would have liked them to went straight to my rack and organised together, because one day I WOULD fit in them.

Clothes carry energy: emotional associations, memories and feelings. It's the reason I still have my Year 6 jumper filled with signatures of classmates I don't see anymore and why somewhere, in a box, I still have a broken necklace with the initial B hanging from its neck.

My skinny pile was accumulating an energy I neither wanted nor benefited from, so one day I decided to do something I am traditionally very bad at doing. I let go. I released the skinny pile.

Anything that could do up and did actually fit me I wore, without concern for how I had initially envisaged myself looking in said pieces. Not skinny enough? Who the fuck cares. I wore piece after piece from my skinny pile and had never felt more empowered. I was reclaiming ownership of an energy that no longer served me and turning it into strength.

Except for that godforsaken white fucking dress. Try as I may, it still wouldn't fit me. So in the week of a show I was styling for Melbourne Fashion Week, I got a phone call from my best friend Tay that changed everything. 'Deni, what the fuck am I supposed to wear to a fashion show? I want to look fierce and make you proud. I'm literally here googling "Kim Kardashian Fashion Show".' Taylah and I share a mutual love for Kim Kardashian and her aesthetic, and while we wear the same size shoe (bestie goals), Tay is easily two dress sizes smaller than I am. At that moment I knew exactly what to do.

'Tay, honey, I have the perfect dress for you. I've never worn it, and it's time someone does.' Tay knew exactly the dress I was referring to; everyone in my orbit knew just how much I loved that dress and how upset I was that it didn't fit.

'But, Deni, I can't, it means so much to you.' She's a true gem of a friend.

'Honey, it's weighing me down. It doesn't fit me, and it's about time someone gave it the outing it truly deserves.'

The following week, after the last model walked the runway, I made my way over to my family and friends who were watching in the crowd with tear-filled eyes. When I got to Taylah in that little white dress I stopped and soaked her in, watching her with awe and pride. She looked positively resplendent in the dress that had plagued me with such insecurity.

In one swift moment, I was taught the power of letting go: the joy and the strength in releasing the things that aren't serving you. Because it isn't until we let go that we can truly sit back and bask in the glory of that release. Sometimes it's a relationship, other times it's a lifestyle, and sometimes it's a little white dress.

Some helpful resources:

National Eating Disorders Collaboration

NEDC is an initiative of the Australian Government dedicated to developing and implementing a system of care for the prevention and treatment of eating disorders. Head to their website for resources, tips and guides curated by people with lived experience.

nedc.com.au

Butterfly Foundation

An incredible organisation I have worked with, offering support for eating disorders and body issues.

butterfly.org.au

Body-positive creators I love to follow on the 'gram:

@allira.potter

@curvysam

@emeliamorrisstylist

@i_weigh

@jameelajamil
@jvn
@katewas_
@katie_parrott
@milohartill
@oliviamollyrogers
@laura.henshaw & @stephclairesmith
@thebodzilla

Affirmation

I am proud of this vessel that carries me through life.

I awe at its strength.
And marvel at its beauty.

I am grateful for it.
I will care for it.
I will honour it.
With empathy, love and kindness.

Thank you, dear vessel, for carrying my spirit.

8.

Home truths

Are you familiar with the biblical story of the prodigal son? If, unlike me, you didn't study the Bible for ten years of your life, let me break it down for you. When old mate JC (Jesus Christ) walked the earth with his twelve apostles in tow, he educated them in the word of God, with stories and parables. This one sits in the Book of Luke.

The story centres on a family of four: a father, mother and their two sons. They were landowners and, by all accounts, wealthy. When the boys hit their late teens, their father sat them down and offered them each half of all of his earnings. The younger son stayed with his father to work on their land, saving his half of the family's wealth. The older, rebellious and altogether more curious son took his half of the earnings and moved out of their farm to wilder pastures.

Over a #hotgirlsummer, the older son proceeded to spend all of his money on the good life. He drank a lot, developed a penchant for sex workers and spent every last cent on live-laugh-loving. So much so that he eventually found himself out on the street, homeless and starving, before finding work as a servant on a pig farm, eating the remnants of food given to the little piggies. He'd hit rock bottom. The older son vowed to return home to his father's farm, apologise for turning his back on his family and offer his services to work on their farm, as a servant.

When he made his way back home, his father couldn't believe his eyes. He'd thought his son was dead but, like Jesus Christ himself, he had come back from the afterlife. The older son started to ask for forgiveness but before he could even finish, his father sent him off to shower, got his servants to dress his son in the finest of robes and threw him a party.

Later that night the younger brother returned home to hear loud music playing and a servant filled him in. Suffice to say that little bro was not impressed, and when he asked his father why he had forgiven so easily, he said, 'Your brother was lost and now he is found. We must celebrate in forgiveness.'

Growing up in the Church and studying this story, I could always relate to the yearning of the prodigal son to make a life for himself away from his provincial home. As I've mentioned, I was a hopeless romantic with wide-eyed dreams of the big city. I spent many an hour daydreaming of cities like Paris and New York and London, fashion meccas that I had seen displayed so fantastically on the silver screen. I knew in my soul that it was where I belonged.

And so I planned my own escape from Geelong, dreaming of wilder pastures, from the age of seven.

In this chapter, we're going to investigate the way in which the concept of 'home' shapes our sense of self from an early age and into our adult lives. We're going to look at how your environment informs the way you live, the people you surround yourself with and your behaviours and the activities in which you participate in. We'll also dissect the micro-adjustments we can make in order to find our way back to the home that is most authentically our own. After all, home is a physical place but it's also an experience, a feeling, a spirit. It's a psychological anchor.

I was fortunate enough to be raised in a tremendously loving home, which, in many ways, was a warm, positive environment. The first house I grew up in has always been my favourite. Humble. Working class. Small and full of soul. Offering shelter and safety. The house was a space that tethered me to my family, to my culture and to my identity.

Memories of my teenage years are punctuated by our family home in the new-at-the-time suburb of Waurn Ponds. My dad built that house with his own hands. It was massive: a double-storey wog castle that my friends dubbed 'The Mansion'. My favourite thing about that house was that my parents converted the spare room into a sewing studio for their aspiring fashion designer son.

I spent so many weekends sewing in that room, a sanctuary from all the bullies at school who made fun of my fashion fantasies. I'd stare up at my wall, which was covered in pages torn from magazines all the way up to the ceiling. Sewing and dreaming of faraway lands, where I might find some of my own Queerness and sense of glamour represented in the spaces around me.

When I made that big leap moving to Paris to study, I found myself out of my comfort zone in so many ways. I genuinely believe that often, in order to truly find yourself, you must throw yourself into uncharted waters. Paris was the whole damn ocean for an eighteen-year-old like me, and I soaked up every damn wave and current. I felt as though I had finally found home.

Then something unexpected happened.

Following my trip to Paris, I met my parents and brother in Austria, where most of my father's family lived, and then we spent the summer travelling across Serbia, my parents' homeland; Bosnia, where my grandparents had a summer house and farm; and Croatia, to the small village my mother was born in. It wasn't the first time I'd been to 'the old country', as my cousins and I called it, but it was the first time I went as a young adult.

A week after landing in Austria, we made our way to Sremska Mitrovica, my parents' home town. I'll never forget the morning my mum took us to the house she was raised in. I'd grown up hearing many times over the story of how my mother, her sister and their thirteen cousins lived between two neighbouring houses. I'd even visited it once before, but this time felt different. I'd forgotten just how small the house was, no wider than most units in Australia. The building was rendered concrete, its old roof tiles looking as though they could really do with an upgrade. The fence was painted dark brown and there was a small fruit tree in the front yard.

I looked at that house and then I looked at my mother. The owner of her cleaning business, alongside my father. A woman who left this house eighteen years prior and made her way out of a soon to be war-torn Former Yugoslavia, to give her future family a better life. I wondered what would have become of her if she had never left, if she had remained in that environment. Living with her misogynistic, alcoholic uncles, undervalued, underappreciated, not given the opportunities Australia had afforded her. My mother's life was the perfect example of when someone is taken out of an underprivileged, abusive environment and introduced to a world of opportunities, making everything suddenly seem possible. In this new world she was able to make her own home, both inwardly and outwardly.

I was so proud in that moment I broke down in tears. Every time I go back to that house, I have the exact same reaction, filled with pride for the woman who gave me life and led by example.

I thought I'd found my heart space in Paris, but it was in this small Serbian village where I would truly start to understand where home really was and what it meant to me.

＊

Have you ever noticed just how much the place we call home can become a personality trait? Celebrities do this all the time. Jenny is from The Bronx. Will is from Philadelphia, born and raised. Gaga is an Italian girl from New York City. Gemma Collins is the Queen of Essex. Jay-Z is from the Marcy Projects and Beyoncé was born in Houston, don't ya know? Take one scroll through TikTok and you'll find Youssra '2200 brother', Aurelia St Clair with her musings on Melbourne's postcodes and a plethora of hot takes on people who live in specific suburbs. I often refer to myself as 'Deni from Geelong' and I'm currently in my 'Barwon Heads Mum' era.

Community spirit is powerful. So often, even long after a person is removed from their community of origin, they will continue to wear it as a badge of honour. They loudly declare their roots as a point of pride, as if to say, 'I am still part of that team.' Jenny and Will no longer live in The Bronx or Philly respectively, but those places are still key identity markers for them.

However, for as many noteworthy people who have worn their 'home' with pride, there are those who discard their origin stories altogether, typically out of shame and a desire to reinvent themselves. During her famed 'German heiress' era, it was never clear where Anna Delvey was *really* from; Coco Chanel embellished the facts of her origin story; and many a famous Brit who hails from Northern England has been forced by their agents to take elocution lessons to sound more 'posh'.

What does home mean to you? In what ways do you identify with or resist the concept?

Sometimes, when humans are asked about this big, complex subject, they will at first mention where they grew up. Others will get even more specific and add emotional descriptors to communicate the feeling of home: 'When I breathe in the peninsula sea breeze, I smell Mount Eliza.'

You might feel that home lives in your memories. Home equates to memories of childhood afternoons at the beach, car trips to the snow, of Christmas morning and chaotic Boxing Day shopping with your mum till you both drop. (Just me? Fuck we love a sale in my house.)

Some of us may identify sentimental landmarks that represent cherished rituals. A tree that you read under. Sitting at the piano. The library you read fashion books in to escape your bullies. The Macca's car park you had your first kiss in. Playing basketball at the park with your brother.

With age, though, your idea of home may get a little deeper and more layered. Home becomes a sanctuary, the place you can go when the outside world is crazy and you really can't be fucked thinking about the passive-aggressive email Janet sent you at work today. It becomes your happy place, a safe space for you to take off your shoes, pour yourself that cocktail, curl up to an episode of *Real Housewives* and drown out Janet and the office for the night, with Kyle Richards and Lisa Rinna, until tomorrow begins. Perhaps you realise that home is in fact wherever you make it, as long as you're surrounded by the people you love.

I heard a centenarian describe home on the internet recently and their description stopped me in my tracks:

'When I think about home, I think what a good life I've had.'

Home truly lives within you, in your mind's eye, at the core of your very spirit.

I want you to think about this for a moment. Maybe take a beat, pull out your notepad and write your answers down to the questions below. I'll be here waiting.

 Over to you, darling

- Where do you feel most at home?
- More importantly, WHY does this feel like home?
- Is home a physical space, is it a person, is it a memory, is it a feeling?
- Speaking of spaces, do you like the physical space in which you currently live?
- Would you say your home space reflects your authentic self?
- Is your bedroom a reflection of your current state of mind?
- Do you take pride in your surroundings? If not, why?
- On the topic of people, with whom do you feel most at home?
- Why do they feel like home?
- Or, on the flip side, why don't they?

- Is home a safe place that you can trust to take comfort in after a long day or during a particularly challenging season of life?
- Do you feel at home within yourself?
- If yes, how do you think you've got there and how can you maintain that?
- If no, why not?

On paper you can have all the ingredients of a warm, safe and loving home environment, and yet still not feel completely at peace. The reason for this is often because you are neither at peace nor at home within yourself.

It's why many make the very 'prodigal son' pilgrimage to backpack around the world, trying to 'find themselves' in the unknown. Honey, I've been there, done that. You can run in search of yourself, from one corner of the globe to another, but it isn't until you sit and make peace within that you will truly find home.

When I was younger, my grandmother would criticise my desire to chase a big career and faraway cities: 'Wouldn't you rather get a good job and build a house with your money?' she'd ask. When I told her, with my teenage rebel gusto, that I honestly couldn't care less whether I ever own a house, she looked at me with shock and horror written all over her face. For most of my childhood and early life, I prioritised life experiences over traditional social expectations. To my teen self, travel and cities with pulsing heartbeats and a robust career in fashion would allow me to make my home. Or so I thought.

What happens when home isn't a safe space, when you can't trust it to keep you warm? During one particularly challenging season of my life, the *Cosmo* office became my home, my solace from the outside world. When I was most unhappy, I'd get to work super early and stay extra late. I came in on weekends, just to sit at my desk and work. I sat on the pink couch, underneath the neon Cosmopolitan sign, for hours many a Sunday, reading the archives of the magazine I was truly honoured to work for. That couch felt like home. The pages of our magazine felt like home. My desk felt like home. My colleagues felt like home.

That office was my home for five incredible years. In retrospect, it was the feeling of security and familiarity that saw me seek refuge in that office when I felt as though my physical home couldn't provide what my soul so desperately craved.

Eventually I reached breaking point and pulled myself out of Sydney, the city I had called home for six years. Making the decision to move back to Geelong after the closing of that chapter was one of the hardest but most necessary decisions I've ever made.

To this day, I'll never forget the way I felt when the plane hit the tarmac at Avalon airport. The way I felt when I stepped off the plane and walked my way through the crisp chill of that Victorian morning air. I was finally home. I felt it deeply, to the bone. My mother was standing at the other end of the arrivals door and upon seeing her face, I felt the feeling wash over me once more. I felt it again driving into our suburb. Walking up the stairs of my family's house. Into my teenage bedroom, as I had left it. I was home and I knew it, and yet for every time I had left Geelong in search of brighter pastures, I couldn't have ever imagined that it would take coming back to find myself once more.

The story of the prodigal son played in my head that night in bed. As I shut my eyes, I said a little prayer to God and thanked him for returning me home safely. I had some ways to go to find my internal home, but my external sanctuary was warm and it was safe. I was ready to do the work.

When I think of humans who have come out of less than fortunate home environments to find strength and peace within themselves, Oprah Winfrey is one human who comes to mind. Born and raised in Mississippi, into a family she describes as poor, and raised largely by a grandmother who abused her, her parents absent: this is a home environment that, on paper, didn't lend itself to the idea that the child who Oprah was would grow up into the billionaire media icon and mogul who she would one day become. Oprah is the perfect example of when someone takes the environment of their lived experience and turns it on its head – though not, it absolutely has to be emphasised, without struggle and resilience and a lot of fucking trauma healing. Oprah vowed to strive for better: to live with intention and empower young women like her to live a life emboldened.

In her acceptance speech for *Variety* Magazine's 'Women in Power' award, Oprah spoke of her boarding school in South Africa. She had long wanted to help educate a group of young women so that they could break the cycle of poverty. She had tried a handful of times to do such work in the US, bringing young women into schools, but she explains that ultimately it wasn't enough. In order for these women to change their mindset, they had to see more permanent changes in their home environments. What she noticed was that when the students she was mentoring returned to their homes, they would inevitably fall back into old habits. This is why she opened a boarding school, so that these young women could be encouraged, around the clock, to live with intention.

This is an extreme example, and not one that is easily replicated for obvious reasons. But it begs the question: how do we break the cycle of home environments (physical spaces, people and feelings) that no longer serve us?

When it comes to this crazy little ride called life, it's a given that there are layers to our lived experience that are completely out of our control, for example our race, the social class we are born into, our sexual orientation, our authentic gender identity, whether or not we are able-bodied, natural disasters, freak accidents, genetic health conditions – I mean, the list could go on. Let's call these the macro factors.

But we also know there are some things that are firmly within our control, whether or not that's easily apparent. Let's call those the micro factors. These can range from the way you choose to set up and style your bedroom to keeping up a daily ritual that sparks joy in your home life, or setting small, seemingly simple personal boundaries in a shared house environment. The thing about the micro factors is they're often so small as to seem invisible within the fabric of our daily lives. But in order to make big changes that allow us to live with intention and positively reshape the larger course of our lives, we must make many a micro-adjustment.

NEVER UNDERESTIMATE THE POWER OF MICRO-ADJUSTMENTS. I cannot stress this enough.

I want you to think about the key factors that are currently impacting your mindset. I can almost assure you they're all environmental, and your environment is the MVP in the flow of your daily life. Let's keep breaking this down.

Over to you, darling

Before we kick off this exercise, if you're at home, I'd like you to find a space that you feel comfortable and most at peace in. A place that will anchor you. If you're not at home, this could still work – the key is that I need you to feel anchored. To help you do that, I want to ease you in with a very simple meditative breathing exercise.

Shut your eyes.

If you are sitting, sit cross-legged with the palms of your hand on each thigh, just before your knee. Then take three deep breaths, in and out.

I want you to repeat this three times over. On the third round, bring up your right hand and place it on your heart. Let your breath and heart and the palm of your hand connect as one so that you feel anchored to where you are and who you are.

Once you've completed this breathwork, slowly open your eyes and return to your surroundings.

Now that you feel anchored, I want you to consider the following:

This is your environment

Where you live, who you live with, the people you surround yourself with, where you work, who you work with, what you choose to do for a living, where you study (if you study). Your digital environment, who you follow on social media. What you listen to and who is speaking to you. What you choose to watch and read and consume every single day. This is all your environment. Is your current environment serving your soul in a positive, peaceful and abundant way?

This is your mindset

Accept that your mindset will absolutely play a role in how you behave, the choices you make, the way you perceive the world, the way you experience life, both physically and emotionally, outwardly and internally.

These are your daily behaviours and activities

... and it is these, my darlings, that affect the outcomes we get in life.

See how it all begins with your environment?

Have you ever found yourself sitting at a desk, feeling stuck for an idea, for inspiration? Maybe you need help writing an email, or a reply to that text message, yet you can't seem to string a single cohesive sentence together. Then suddenly, you're in the fucking shower and BOOM, the perfect response, idea, paragraph, moment of inspiration, drops into your mind. Because you changed your environment, honey: you're at peace, the water is running, you're void of negative environmental factors clouding your vision.

The second I set foot on 'home' soil in Geelong after those long, hard days towards the end of my life in Sydney, I gained perspective like never before. The same can be said for my coming-out journey. There's been some discussion of the correlation between global lockdowns and the rising rates of humans coming out as trans and non-binary. The outside world pressed pause, and in the safety of my parents' home, I finally felt as though I could connect with who I most authentically was without fear of judgement. Alone with our thoughts, we reconnected with our true spirit. It was less about the physical spaces we occupied than the absence of external noise that suddenly made way for internal clarity.

That, my darlings, is what home is all about. Going to sleep each night, no matter where I am, or who might be there by my side, knowing in my mind and in my soul exactly who I am. That is the motherfucking destination I had been searching for my whole life.

Despite all the years spent in Paris, Serbia, London and Sydney, it was in Geelong where I learnt to piece all the parts of the puzzle together. And when I was ready to look outside of myself at my surroundings in the place I'd grown up, ironically it was all the things I had grown up hating about Geelong that I now found myself falling in love with: its small-town mentality, everybody-knows-everybody's-business nature, its obsession with community sports. I now saw support, community, charm, warmth and an open heart.

These things no longer threatened my identity because I now knew exactly who I was. It's the reason I've never felt more at home in my own company. Being alone with my thoughts is treasured time for me. It's no coincidence that, when I think back to Little Deni, they always felt that way too. It was when I was alone in my sewing room, or alone in the library at school or alone wandering the streets of London, that I always felt most content. Most at peace. Most at home.

I want you to get thinking about this at a very fundamental level. Is your current environment serving you? How is your environment impacting your mindset and therefore informing your daily behaviour and the choices you make? Are you searching for home in the eyes of others or do you, in your soul, feel at home?

If the answer to that final question is no, I want you to think about the micro-adjustments you can make to change that, knowing that with the accumulation of many micro-adjustments comes serious macro change.

Some of you might be sceptical. Let's explore this with some hypotheticals for a moment, shall we?

Hypothetical #1

You're a creative at heart, always have been. Art and colour and freedom of expression make the hairs on your neck stand up, in the best way. But you work in corporate finance because your parents told you artists don't earn money, and so you completed your commerce degree begrudgingly at the same uni all your girlfriends went to. Five years later, you're sitting in a work meeting listening to your boss, Richard, talk about negative gearing, and all you want to do is throw the nearest stapler at him. And at your parents, and at your girlfriends who told you commerce would be 'so fun, babe, and plus we'll get jobs that pay us so much money you can just buy art'.

Possible micro-adjustment

Put the stapler down and take a deep breath.

Sweetie, enrol yourself in an art class immediately, a night one. Fuck, if that's too much of a commitment for you, swing by Officeworks on your way home and buy yourself one of those big portfolio books that we used in high school. The paper with no lines. As well as a set of coloured pencils. Then go crazy.

Once you've given that a whirl, why not stop by an art supply store next month and buy yourself a canvas and some paint, choose a brush that feels like magic in your hands. Go home, pour yourself a wine and paint to your heart's content. No one's saying you should quit your job (yet), no one's pressuring you to become the next Andy Warhol (yet); just go and start with some after-work art activity to reinvigorate that passion and reunite you with your inner child.

Who knows what might come of it? Worst case, you'll have some sick paintings to hang in your house. Best case, you'll reinvigorate your true calling and quit your fucking job.

Hypothetical #2

You're a Queer human living in a regional town. You've only just come out to your family and, well, it didn't go down so well. You binged *Heartstopper* in a weekend and wish with everything in your power that you could have had a similar adolescent experience. Your heart's in your throat whenever you see gay couples on the street walk hand in hand; you long for any kind of intimacy. There are few fellow Queers in the village, and quite honestly Grindr intimidates the fuck out of you. You really want to start wearing nail polish but you fear the looks you'll get from Dave at the office. You can't even pick up at the pub on

Friday night because everyone is straight, and honestly are you supposed to live like that?

Possible micro-adjustment

Take a deep breath and look for your nearest LGBTQIA+ peer support group. Can I suggest googling QLife? Start online, then slowly but surely make your way out into the community, and into the real world. Your parents may never support you, or with time they may become your greatest allies – just know that, regardless of the outcome, your community will support you. You may not have had a gay youth, but honey, you will have a gay life.

As for that nail polish, why don't you start with painting just the one nail. Seriously. Try it. Then maybe jump to two. Before you know it, you'll be a local at your Westfield nail salon and honestly who cares what Dave thinks. You will love and be loved, greatly, I promise. You will pick up all the humans and have all the sex and this will all be a distant memory soon, but right now I want you to take your Queer journey one micro-adjustment at a time.

Hypothetical #3

Your alarm hasn't even gone off yet and you can already hear Isabella singing into the television downstairs. Bella's six and she still misses her dad, so you let her off the hook this morning when you make your way into the kitchen to make yourself a coffee. You sit outside and light up the first of many cigarettes you'll have that day as you contemplate your life.

How did you get here? You were married, he was perfect, your high school sweetheart who made a child with you and then he fucked Christina, got her pregnant, started drinking every night and left you and Bella for her and theirs.

Who even are you anymore? You haven't felt like yourself since the split three years ago. You haven't moved on. Not even close. You've barely touched yourself in the same time. Your friends keep telling you to just download Tinder.

Meanwhile, your shitty job and single income are making it harder to make ends meet each day. You think, for a moment, that maybe this is all too hard.

Possible micro-adjustment

Take three deep breaths. Then close your eyes and think about three words that describe how you currently feel. Write them down. Tonight I want you to think about three things in your life that you are proud of. Write those down. Tomorrow morning I want you to think about three things you are grateful for. Write them down. Repeat this exercise every day for a week. Then another.

Following that I'd like you to make yourself an appointment with your GP and ask to be put on the mental health treatment plan we discussed earlier, which will give you therapy appointments subsidised by Medicare. I want you to ask for a referral to a femme-presenting therapist who can talk you through the grief and trauma you're currently tackling.

But you don't have to do everything at once. Start with the journal. This will help you compartmentalise your thoughts and feelings on a micro level, so that you can work through them.

I also want you to make time for yourself. Leave Bella with someone you trust to care for her occasionally, get yourself a massage, go get your hair done, buy yourself a vibrator online. Hug yourself in the shower and tell that woman you love her. Reconnect with the woman you are. She's in there and it's about time she comes out. Not all at once: one step at a time.

That's the thing about micro-adjustments. You might not make all the changes straight away, but honey, you will feel all at once when these big internal changes are making an impact. That I can assure you.

When you do find home within, please, for the love of Jesus and Gaga, protect it at all costs. Keep it safe from threat and harm. Nurture it. Care for it. Converse with it. Check in with it. Love it deeply and with great respect and admiration. Set its boundaries. Keep it filled with your spirit. Keep it warm and cosy. Wrap the metaphorical doona around yourself, because home is your most prized possession and home is you.

I understand that there is great privilege in the ability to generate such change within our lives, and I don't acknowledge that lightly. But whenever I have found myself to be schlepping down Struggle Street with sweat dripping down my back, I remind myself that if my mum could do it, I can do it too. If my Romani Gypsy nomad Traveller ancestors could do it, then heaven knows that I can do it too. And if I, the non-binary, gay son of migrants, born and raised in Geelong and never having had a silver spoon in my mouth, can do it, I assure you that you can too. Because you have strength beyond your own knowing.

Did I just fist-bump in the air? You bet I did.

So can I just say I am very fucking excited that you are making your way closer to home, the home that lives inside of you. We're getting to the pointy end now.

Dance break

'Empire State of Mind' – Jay-Z (feat. Alicia Keys)

Jay-Z is my favourite recording artist and New York City is my favourite place in the world, so imagine my delight and surprise when this song came out, a celebration of the city I so desperately wanted to call home. Until one day it dawned on me that if New York is a state of mind, we all have our own version of 'New York', a fantastical place that seems out of reach, a place we are convinced we'd be eternally happy in. I have visited New York twice and one day I will live there, but what I have taken away from each trip is that no matter where I am, I can sprinkle a little New York energy into my daily life via my mindset, the very thing that controls my actions and behaviours.

Thirty laps around the sun

In that difficult time towards the end of my Sydney years, I had another full-circle moment – much like when I'd visited my parents' Serbian village – in a different part of the world that reminded me home is a concept that can transcend time and place.

Growing up, I knew the names of the Romani tribes both my mother and father belonged to and was proud to learn that we had come from this long, proud lineage of people. When I was eight years old, one of my great-uncles came to visit us from Canada. I remember him being very brown skinned, darker than any of my other uncles. During one of many family lunches we had with him, the men in my family started discussing our own origin story. We knew that we spoke a dialect of Romanian, and that somewhere along the line our ancestors spent some time there, but we were never certain that Romania was where our story began.

My great-uncle informed this full house of eager listeners that he had done some research on our ancestry, and his findings traced us back to India. Many of my relatives are dark-skinned, so this made a lot of sense. Many of us have at some point in our lives been mistaken as South Asian.

Twenty-two years later, I boarded a plane to Mumbai. My boyfriend was going there on a work trip and we'd decided I would come along as the trip coincided with my thirtieth birthday. I was grateful that I finally had the chance to make my way to this country I had been obsessing over since my great-uncle had revealed this glimmer of family history.

On our second day in India, while my boyfriend was busy at work, I took myself into the town of Pune where we were staying, located to the south of Mumbai. The first place I went to was a local market, because in my travels I have found that markets are always the heartbeat of many foreign destinations. What I saw took my breath away and filled my eyes with tears.

I looked around at the locals and in their eyes saw my own. I saw the eyes of my parents and grandparents and uncles and aunties and cousins and became covered in goosebumps. What's more, as I walked through the stalls, many of the market folk began greeting me in their native tongue. When I informed them that I only spoke English, they told me they thought I'd been travelling from northern India. When I got back to our hotel room that night I called my parents immediately to tell them all about it.

(Sidenote: during the lockdowns of 2020, my family, like so many others, ordered an AncestryDNA kit online. A whole lot of saliva and twelve weeks later, our results returned, and it turned out our great-uncle was right. My family are descendants of the Romani Gypsy people by way of northern India, specifically the Punjab region. They had moved their way from the Punjab, down through Africa via Egypt, up and over to the Middle East, before landing in the Balkans.)

And so it was that on the eve of my thirtieth birthday, I sat alone by the hotel pool and made a list of all the things I'd been proud to achieve in my thirty laps around the sun alongside a list of the things I wanted to achieve in the next year of my life. One of them was to finally find myself, another to make a home for myself. I knew that to do this I would need to get out of that relationship with my partner. It would take me a further year and a half to do so, but in that moment, the sun beaming down on my face, I knew I had to break it off.

It took going halfway across the world, to a country I had never been before, to finally arrive at the destination of my internal home.

Affirmation

No matter how lost I may feel, I will continue to remind
    myself that home is within me.
The most sacred of places.

I honour my home.
I love my home.

I am grateful for its warmth and safety.
I am grateful for its protection.

And I will protect it forevermore.
With honour and gratitude.

9.

Spirituality, surrender and devotion

S pirituality can be an incredibly divisive concept. Even the mere mention of it can get the eyeballs of many a human rolling into the back of their head. To some it's a way of life, a sacred energy source that has the power to anchor you, to steer you in the right direction and provide a great sense of security in the knowledge that there is a higher power guiding you. To others, it's nonsensical, a 'woo-woo' money-making scheme selling you crystals, a manifestation journal, some tarot cards perhaps and a $300 psychic reading.

I'm not sure where on the spectrum of these thoughts you sit, but as we edge our way to the end of this book, I'm going to invite you to approach this chapter with an open mind. I think it's important to state up-front that spirituality and religion are two very separate concepts, even though they're often lumped together – which is partly why, I think, the bad rap from religion deters humans from spirituality. I would love you to check your ego at the door, along with any preconceived notions you may have of spirituality as a whole, because when I tell you that spirituality has been the most important pillar of my life, I mean it. Surrender to this chapter.

In order to know who you are and why you're here, it's important to connect with spirit: the spirit that is your own and the power in spirit that guides you.

In my conversations with Elise about spirituality, she says that, to her way of thinking and feeling, spirituality is the remembrance that you are never alone.

Let me say that again.

Spirituality is the remembrance that you are never alone.

I have never truly felt alone. I have always felt connected to spirit. As a child, I spent a lot of time talking to myself, sometimes out loud, knowing that someone was listening. I asked for help. For advice. I spoke of my wildest dreams and ambitions and had a deep knowing that what I saw in my mind for the future had already happened, it was locked in. I just had to bring it to life. I never once doubted that I would work in fashion or live abroad or fall in love or be successful. My intuition always knew.

Who exactly was I speaking to? I imagine you might be sitting there thinking, 'Well, all children talk to themselves, Deni', but let me assure you, I'm not talking about talking to imaginary friends or a stuffed toy. I'm talking about a spiritual support group I knew I always had. I thought everyone felt this way, but I found out much later in life that's not the case.

I've also, for as long as I can remember, had really vivid dreams where I could remember every minor detail. As a teenager I started to dissect them via Google: any time I would dream about an animal or a very unique detail, colour, message, I was curious to know its meaning. I thought everyone dreamt that vividly.

As a religious child and teenager, I began to address that power as God. It made sense to me. I prayed each night and God listened to my prayers, often answering them overnight. Whenever I felt as though I needed a little extra support, I reached out to God more so than usual. It's pretty common that when people are going 'through it', whether they are of faith or not, they will look to the heavens and ask – 'why now, God, why me?'

Elise says that even she tends to be most spiritual when faced with hard moments in life. Humans are wired up to feel as though we need guidance. We are brought into the world and nursed until we can speak for ourselves. It should be no surprise then that as adults, when something is not going to plan, we look up for help.

But it is the lack of support we feel we receive in return that typically turns people away from spirit, or at least what they believe to be 'spirit'. If God is real, for example, why did he take my uncle away at the age of seventeen, or let my best friend commit suicide at twenty-three; why does he sit back and watch as millions of humans struggle the world over every day? We become disappointed by these variables and find ourselves questioning our very existence.

Did you know that the most common times humans book in to see a psychic are after a breakup or the death of a loved one? It's no surprise that the common thread in those situations is loss and grief: when we lose something we love, we in turn feel lost ourselves, desperate for answers.

But what I urge you to understand is that the answer to most of life's scariest questions are within you, via the universe. You just have to listen to the whisper.

Listening to your intuition is the key to living an authentic life. This is another way of framing a situation I have been talking about since way back in the first chapter of this book: your intuition has guided you since childhood, and the further we walk away from it the less authentic our lives become.

My family stopped 'studying the Bible' and being active members of the Jehovah's Witness church after I came out as gay, and for a very long time after that, I stopped praying. Even in some of my darkest times, it was prayer that I most turned to, even though I wasn't sure God was 'listening'. It took me a while to understand why I kept praying: I didn't have the language yet to make sense of it all.

I'm sure that now, if you are within arm's reach of a smartphone, a regular user of social media or simply an active consumer of pop culture, you will be familiar with terms that fall under the umbrella of spirituality: 'the Universe', 'calling out', boundaries, manifestation, affirmations and intention-setting. You might be aware of more tangible practices like vision boards, gratitude journals and meditation. You might have noticed that crystals are at an all-time peak in trend, people are buying tarot cards at a rapid rate and anyone with the Co-Star app can break down their birth chart and tailor their moon, sun and rising signs to their personality traits (or vice versa). While all these can be incredible tools to connect you to spirit, Elise says they are not necessarily integral to your own spiritual journey.

My spiritual journey truly started to kick in for me in Sydney via my dear friend and fellow author Stacey June. Stacey and I met during my time at *Cosmo*. We both worked in media, me at the magazine and Stacey in radio and podcasting. I had styled her for a magazine shoot and the day I met Stacey on set, I was going through a particularly turbulent time in my relationship. Her energy grounded me and within ten minutes of us making conversation during hair and make-up, we became fast friends. I've been fortunate enough to make lifelong friendships with a handful of my styling clients over the years, but I remember feeling as though Stacey and I had been dropped into each other's lives for a reason. As though it were divine intervention.

For the remainder of my time in Sydney, both Stacey and I would go through one life-changing season after another, never further than a phone call away for support. Stacey and her husband, Ben, became two of my strongest anchors in that city. I would visit them fortnightly at their serene home in Coogee for dinner. It was during these catch-ups that Stacey began sharing with me the very spiritual side to her identity.

Both Stacey and Ben lived with great intention. They meditated and did yoga, they had a holistic kinesiologist and life coaches, they had affirmations and intentions written on post-it notes stuck all over their house. I had never met anyone quite like them and I was in awe.

(For those unaware, holistic kinesiology is a practice that uses muscle testing said to balance our body's energy systems, drawing on practices such as traditional Chinese acupuncture. As our bodies trap trauma, kinesiology aims to release that negative energy our body all too often holds on to, not dissimilar to reiki healing.)

Over a green curry one evening, Stacey introduced me to the practice of great surrender. I was venting to Stacey about the unravelling-at-the-seams nature of my relationship at the time. Unsure of how much longer life could be breathed into it, she turned to me while cooking and said, 'Den, you know the solution to this problem. The answers to your question. They're within you. Why don't you surrender it to the universe and listen to what it tells you?'

Surrender. The universe. What was she talking about?

The concept of the 'law of attraction' started trending around the time that Oprah covered *The Secret*, the worldwide bestselling book, on her talk show. Somehow, surprisingly, being the Oprah fanatic that I am, I must have missed those episodes. Stacey spoke to me about how we attract the energy we put into the world. Toxic energy comes back to us as a result of a lack of boundaries, and what we choose to accept as appropriate treatment and behaviour.

Energy, my darling reader, is currency. You must be very protective of whom you choose to invest your energy in and whose energy you choose to receive. Sometimes it can be difficult to navigate energies you feel as though you are forced to take on, in spaces like your place of work or school, or even within the walls of your family home. But how you filter that energy is in your control. The ways in which you set boundaries with this energy and navigate it so as to not let it harm your own is very much in your control – if you are ready to take control and want it to be.

Have you ever found yourself dropping to your knees at a crossroads moment, desperate for an answer to guide you in choosing a direction? My biggest crossroads moments happened during my Saturn return. For context, at around the same time I had met Stacey, we ran a feature in our magazine about this globally trending topic. A Saturn return is an astrological event that occurs every twenty-seven to twenty-nine-and-a-half years, when the planet Saturn returns to the sign and degree that it was at when you were born. This age is typically associated with major life changes, like changes in your career, breakups, engagements and relocations.

Now, you can say what you want about astrology, but what I'll say is that I'm an Aries, through and through. While I have a

Libra Moon and a Capricorn Rising, I'm an Aries Sun and it is in many ways the reason I am the way I am. What do Lady Gaga, Celine Dion, Jonathan Van Ness and Victoria Beckham have in common? They are all Aries, the strongest sign of the zodiac. It's no surprise to me that I share the same sign as these individuals who have experienced their lives play out on stage, both literally and metaphorically; individuals who are driven by passion, living their most authentic lives.

I have also always felt a connection to both astrology and numerology. I was twenty-two when the divine number 11 and thereafter the 11:11 phenomenon began following me. So when the Saturn return feature made its way around the office, it didn't surprise me to discover that all of my life's greatest changes up to that point had occurred from the ages of twenty-seven to thirty.

What's so special about 11:11?

So you've just checked the time on your phone and you see 11:11. You've parked your car and the parking space is numbered 11. You might be on the bus, thinking about a crossroads moment in your life, begging for a sign from somewhere that you are on the right track, and someone walks onto the bus wearing a sports jersey with the number 11 on it. These are all things that began happening to me while living in London. I kept seeing the number 11 and I had no idea what it meant, until my housemate Michelle explained its significance to me.

When you see numbers repeated in combinations such as 111, 222, 333, 444, 555 and so forth, pay attention!

According to the tenets of numerology, these numbers are wake-up calls and signs from your soul and the universe.

Adherents of numerology will tell you that the number 11 is considered to be the 'master number'. It signifies intuition, insight and enlightenment. When paired together as 11 11, that's a clear message from the universe that you need to become more conscious of your surroundings. In some darker times in my life, the number 11 completely disappeared from my orbit. After my breakup in Sydney and my decision to return to Geelong, when I checked into my flight for Avalon the morning I left, I noticed my seat number on my boarding pass. 11D. The number 11 and my initial. I burst into tears. The universe was taking me home and the number 11 was back in my sight.

I was on the right path. Such is the power of connecting to spirit and making sure that you are remaining open to receiving and reading the signs that you encounter.

Oprah often says that the universe is always trying to get your attention. Whispering to you. The key is to listen to those whispers before they become too quiet or impossible to decode. The universe is full of signs, every day, if you are willing to look and listen.

The issue is that we can be quite vague when asking for guidance from the universe. That night in Stacey's kitchen, she taught me about being truly intentional.

While I was initially unfamiliar with the practice of 'setting intentions', I soon realised that I had spent most of my life intention-setting at every turn. Writing my goals down. Sticking them on my wall. Praying. Calling things out loud into the abyss, waiting patiently for them to manifest. I had done this from as young as seven, from when I saw the Eiffel Tower on the television at my auntie's house, to my jobs at *British Vogue* and *Cosmo Australia*. I'd even manifested the boyfriend I was currently contemplating breaking up with as I sat there in Stacey's kitchen. I had walked around Sydney for nine months manifesting a partner like the buff gay men I saw on the streets of Potts Point, Darlinghurst and Surry Hills.

Being able to overlay an existing language and framework onto this practice that I'd long intuitively felt was liberating. But what I realised at the same time was that, over the course of this relationship, my intentional life – the manifestation and positive visualisation; talking to myself in an empowering way – had stopped. I'd stopped seeking my spiritual support system.

Stacey explained to me that in order to surrender a decision to the universe, you must be first ready to relinquish control and have faith that the universe will guide you. Her second bit of advice was that you needed to be specific, both in your question and in the sign you ask the universe to show you. She wasn't talking about anything woo-woo or metaphorical here, we were talking about legitimate physical signs. The more specific the better. You give the universe a timeframe – typically more than a day but no more than three – to really show up for you, and then you switch off.

The key to surrendering is to be truly ready. If you're listening and looking, those whispers are always there, and they will show up when you least expect them to. If I'm honest, I wasn't yet at that moment ready to surrender my relationship's fate to the universe, so I stayed in it for a year longer than I should have.

My moment of surrender came with deep sadness and great realisation. It was a Sunday morning; I was sitting alone in my partner's backyard while he was out having coffee with a friend. I knew that if I stayed in this relationship, it would drain the very little energy I had left. I didn't know who to turn to; I was too embarrassed to turn to my friends or family. So I turned to watching the Oprah Network and stumbled upon a video of Dr Maya Angelou talking about letting go of love and loving someone from afar. Her words stopped me in my tracks:

'Love liberates. It doesn't bind. Love says I love you. I love you if you're across the world or across town. I would like to have you by my side but that's not possible now, so go.'

In that moment I was almost certain it was time for me to go. No matter how much I loved my boyfriend, we were no longer serving each other. We hadn't been for quite some time.

Even so, I needed a sign that I was doing the right thing by leaving.

At that moment I heard Stacey's advice ring in my head: 'Surrender your decision to the universe.' So I said, out loud, 'Universe, I surrender this decision to you. I feel as though it's time for me to leave, but I need you to show me a sign that my intuition is right.'

I chose a very specific sign. Have you ever listened to the lyrics of 'Firework' by Katy Perry? The song begins by asking the listener about the hopeless, aimless feeling of being a plastic bag drifting in the wind, wanting to start again. I wanted to start again, desperately. I yearned for it. So that became my sign. If the universe wanted me to leave, it would show me a plastic bag drifting through the wind. I would give it two days to show up so I could surrender to its power.

Short of three hours later, I found myself walking to a park close to my boyfriend's house, killing time before he came home. I needed to clear my head. As I approached the park, I saw a great big tree. The kind of tree that sweeps over you when you sit at its trunk. I sat by the trunk and looked out over the park, reflecting on how I'd got to that point.

I heard a rustle in the leaves above and then saw a plastic bag emerging from its leaves. In fact, it was a sleeping bag, a poly/plastic blend, drifting gracefully out of the top of this tree before landing directly next to me on the ground. It happened in what felt like slow motion. It took me a couple of seconds to piece the puzzle together: a sleeping bag, made from plastic, had just drifted its way through a gust of wind to land by my side.

I determined that the universe had showed up for me in three hours. I knew what I had to do.

I returned to my boyfriend's house, where he was sitting in the backyard alone, and I proceeded to end our relationship over the next two hours. Tears streamed down both our faces and we held each other tighter than we ever had before, both knowing that this time was final. It was time for me to go. When I arrived back in Geelong the following day, I made a vow to myself that I would reconnect with spirit.

So how do you even start to navigate a relationship with spirituality? I can hear your thoughts, questions and anxieties through the pages, but never fear, darling: I got you.

In retrospect, my capacity to reconnect with spirit – and by extension reconnect with both myself and the world around me – was restored when I started therapy, which allowed me to begin releasing what no longer served me. Therapy was my MVP. Full disclosure, though: there were many bumps along the way, bumps that included sleeping with my ex the next time I went to Sydney for work. Not my finest hour. Other bumps involved drinking too much, partying too hard and meaningless sex to fill the void.

No, my reconnecting with spirit didn't come all at once; rather, it came through many micro-adjustments to my life and environment and daily routine. When you start to do an emotional inventory of who you surround yourself with and investigate the ways in which you exert your energy, it becomes increasingly easier to set boundaries. What I found, in starting this process, was that just like the laws of attraction will tell you, my energy started to attract like energies: humans and work and relationships that served me.

Around this time, a very close friend of mine, Robbie, told me about Elise. Geelong is the sort of city that is just small enough to feel like a town and like any place that has a small-town feel, when people are truly good at what they do, word gets around fast. Robbie spoke to me of his life-changing sessions with Elise, who, as you'll recall, is a reiki healer with credentials in psychology who specialises in trauma healing. Robbie had kindly put my name on her waitlist, and six months later, shortly after another visit to Sydney and a particularly emotional reunion with my ex, I was booked to see Elise.

It was a Saturday morning, and I was hungover as hell from one too many tequilas the night before, but there was no way I was going to cancel this appointment. And I'm glad I didn't. Elise was all the things I had heard her to be. Her presence instantly calmed me, and over the course of our hour-and-a-half-long session, she exceeded my expectations on both the psych front and spiritual side. I held back tears. In that chair, on a morning when I felt as though my light switch was very much turned off, Elise saw the light inside me and urged me to turn it back on: to start with healing and to live intentionally once more.

Four weeks after my appointment with Elise, it was March 2020. Yes, we're going back there. Let's take a minute and take a deep breath in and out, shall we?

At that time, it felt as though in one swift moment the world as we had come to know it was changing irrevocably. But as I've said in earlier chapters, along with lockdowns and mandates and so much fear came the gift of time.

I surrendered my decision to come out as non-binary to the universe, this time choosing purple hearts as my sign. The universe showed me purple hearts in droves over a twenty-four-hour period. Coming out as non-binary was a deeply spiritual experience in and of itself.

Second to my gender journey, the most significant and special thing to come out of that first lockdown for me was the gift of reconnecting with spirit. I dedicated time to it. Serious time. I enrolled into a program Elise runs called 'The Practice'. Think a gym membership but for your spirit and soul. Every fortnight I would eagerly jump into the Zoom webinars she hosted and we would dive into spiritual practice and conversation, learning about healing, meditation, inner-child work and living with great intention.

One exercise in particular left a deep impression on me: 'shadow work affirmations', a form of healing and intention-setting that requires great surrender and acceptance.

Over to you, darling

In one of our first webinars, Elise asked us to take one piece of A4 paper and draw a line straight down the middle. On the left side of the page, she asked us to write down five things that were causing us distress, discomfort or anxiety. These could range from things that were weighing down our mental health and spirit right in that moment, or bigger-picture things that weighed us down. This was our shadow section of the page.

On the right side of the page, Elise taught us to take the shadow feeling and turn it into a positive intention. So, for example, in my shadow section I wrote a very vulnerable, honest and raw feeling that often kept me up at night: *Will I ever have the freedom to truly be authentically who I am?*

Over on the right side, Elise's session allowed me to reframe that shadow feeling into a positive intention: *Universe, I thank you in advance for blessing me with the freedom to live authentically as I am. I am grateful for the liberation that comes with my authentic identity.*

I would love to invite you to do the same exercise. Go find a piece of blank paper and come back with a pen.

Step 1

At the top of your page, write *SHADOW INTENTIONS* and today's date.

Step 2

Run your pen down the centre of the page, so you have two columns.

Step 3

Your left side is your shadow side. Here, I'd like you to write five feelings currently lurking in your spirit's shadows. It could be an anxiety, a fear, a stress, an insecurity, a discomfort, anger, etc. It could be a broader feeling you have long felt, for example:

I fear I am unlovable.
What if I never fall in love?
I don't fit in with my family.
My brother will never accept me for who I am.
I can't come out of the closet.
I am unhappy in my marriage.

Or it might be a feeling that is occupying your mind in this very moment, month, week, day, season of life. For example:

I don't like my vessel this week.
I feel disconnected from my partner this month.
I don't feel valued at work right now.

Step 4

On the right side of the page, you're going to reframe each of your shadows with an affirming or positive action-based intention. You are going to speak this out to the universe, honouring its presence in your life, and you're going to give yourself a statement that feels definitive. I'll reframe some of the above as well as a couple more as examples:

I fear I am unlovable.

TURNS INTO: *Universe, I know that I am worthy of great love, and I thank you in advance for blessing me with its presence in my life.*

What if I never fall in love?

TURNS INTO: *Universe, I trust in your divine timing and I have faith that when the timing is right I will be surrounded with the love I have for so long craved. I thank you in advance for this blessing.*

I can't come out of the closet.

TURNS INTO: *Universe, I ask you to honour me with liberation and the strength to step into my authentic identity on my own terms. Irrespective of what the world thinks, I will honour who I am, and I thank you for the resilience you protect me with.*

I am unhappy in my marriage.

TURNS INTO: *Universe, I thank you in advance for honouring me with the strength to honour my happiness. I will take control of the things that are in my power and walk towards a life that rewards my spirit with joy. Whatever that may look like, I trust in your guidance.*

I don't feel valued at work right now.

TURNS INTO: *I thank you, universe, for leading me towards a position in which I am valued, greatly, for the work I do every day. I thank you for workspaces that foster such cultures.*

Step 5
Once you have each of your shadow intentions written out, stick these on your wall, somewhere you'll see them every day. Perhaps in your bedroom, or on the back of your toilet door (yes, seriously, I've seen people do this).

Step 6
This is the best part. It's time to read these out, loud and proud. Three times consecutively. The first time you'll feel a little timid. The second time you'll start to get it, and the third time you'll say it with great conviction. Feel these intentions in your bones, see them in your mind. You are calling out, practising gratitude and visualising all at once. Such is the power of manifesting with intention.

Do you know how powerful it feels to say such a thing out loud? I became intoxicated with how it made me feel. Slowly, then all at once, it felt as though my light switch had finally turned on and I had all the time in the world to invest in my spirit once more.

I made goals again. I wrote list after list of the things I wanted to attract, and the universe, honey, it started dropping those things into my life one by one. I went old school and dug up *The Secret* movie to watch for the first time. While it gives slight Danoz Direct infomercial vibes in certain spots, it's a great beginner's crash course in positive visualisation and manifesting.

I practised gratitude daily. I meditated. I learned all about crystals and worked with them in my meditation practice. I made vision boards again. I literally covered my walls in them; they even went a little viral on Instagram. I reminded myself with visualisation and daily affirmations that what I wanted would be mine when it was meant to be.

I sat in the shadows. I started to listen to the whispers again. I threw myself into creative endeavours and dedicated my time to me. It's what led me to this moment, to living as an out and proud trans non-binary human. It led me to a career in content creation and storytelling, after the epiphany that my passions extended far beyond fashion alone. It led me to becoming a self-love ambassador, to podcasting and to writing a goddamn book. A 'dream' I've had since Melina Marchetta's *Looking for Alibrandi* moved me deeply at the tender age of fifteen. Every one of those moments led me to this one and will lead me to the next one, and it all began by reconnecting with healing and spirit.

Healing can only begin after making peace with our shadow because healing is not about becoming the best version of yourself. Healing entails letting all the versions of ourselves, even the 'worst' ones, be loved. When we get to a place where we show empathy to every version of ourselves, even those that we are ashamed of, that's when we know we are walking down the path of true healing.

When I asked Elise for her advice to share with anyone who wants to develop their own sense of spirituality, she started with this comment: 'For anyone who doesn't resonate with or connect with spirituality, let's start with an understanding that you don't have to be spiritual per se; this is about having an enquiring mind that connects the dots.'

For me, this is a key foundational point when it comes to the journey I'm encouraging you to embark upon with this book. Speaking for myself, I have always been curious to connect the dots of my identity formation. Whether this involved digging back through intergenerational trauma, unpacking my Queerness or connecting the dots of my cultural identity, I never understood people who were satisfied with just coasting through life. If there is a particular behaviour, emotion, energy or pattern in your life that seems to be holding you back from truly living authentically, there's likely a reason behind it. Get curious and investigate!

Elise continued by saying that the role spirituality plays in her life is knowing that there is a purpose: a conversation with the universe that says, 'I may not have the answer right now but I am looking to you for the solution.' If you're currently experiencing a moment of great difficulty, I want you to remember that, while you may not have the answers right now, the universe has the solution. But you must be open to receiving it, even if that draws you out of your comfort zone.

On great surrender, Elise reflects on her own Saturn return and the moments where she too was brought to her knees, willing to surrender this change to the universe. What Elise values most about surrender is the vulnerability of the moment, when the masks that we put on every day drop and we allow ourselves to be truly raw. The power in vulnerability is unlike anything

I've ever experienced. It is within those moments that I find the greatest of resilience and revelations begin.

When I asked Elise for some tangible tips I can give you here today, her answer took my breath away: 'Spirituality is devotion. Devotion is love. Spirituality is devotional love in action. When you send out devotion into this world, you are sending out love.'

Look for ways to be actively devotional. Some call this gratitude, which is a great place to start, but Elise says that spirituality is at its core a devotional practice. Find daily moments of devotion so that anything you worship becomes your temple. This could be a dance class, a walk alone in the park, taking fifteen minutes each morning to sit alone with your thoughts, to practise gratitude and simply feel the sun on your nose.

Finding your devotional practice could mean investing time in your passions. In fact, in our conversation about this, Elise said to me, 'Deni, there is a great devotion in your fashion. When I see your fashion and the role it plays in your life, that feels spiritual to me.' That comment later made me cry because Elise was absolutely right. I suddenly thought about the seventeen-year-old Deni who devoted their life to sewing and immersing themselves wholeheartedly in fashion. That daily practice saved me. It made me feel at home. It made me feel valued. It poured love into me because I poured love and worship into it.

Worship. Love. Devotion. This is spiritual practice. As you exercise this daily devotion, that action becomes self-devotion: without even realising it at first, you are devoting time and energy to yourself, and energy is what? Currency, honey. And it is invested how? Wisely!

Pouring that devotion into daily practice for yourself is where self-devotion makes way for self-love. While you can use crystals and cards and their like as tools to connect you to spirit, remember that the method doesn't matter so much as making sure that these practices are underpinned by love, worship and devotion.

If I can give you my own lived-experience advice, I would start here:

LIVE WITH GREAT INTENTION.

I want you to start with even just three small intentions this week. On three of the seven days, allocate yourself five minutes to sit in silence with your spirit. Listen to it. What does it want out of that day? What does it need in order to fill your cup? Once you've narrowed down what you want to feel in that moment, say it out loud three times.

This is exactly how I started in lockdown. I'd shut my eyes and choose three intentions for my day. These words summarised how I wanted to feel at that very moment. Say, for example, 'Productive. Creative. Balanced.' And then I would say out loud:

Universe, I thank you in advance for the productivity of today. For blessing me with creativity whilst also allowing my day to sit in a balance. I am blessed and grateful for the productivity, creativity and balance today brings me.

Notice how I speak in the future tense, knowing that the things I have intended are already to be. I've been doing the same thing here before I start writing every one of these chapters. I shut my eyes and I pray to the universe and thank them in advance for letting the words flow out of me. Even though I know it will at times be tough, and I acknowledge the discomfort it may bring, I surrender myself to the process, knowing that I will be blessed with abundance and words that (hopefully) inspire and resonate.

If speaking out loud like this feels weird to you – if anything I am saying feels a little too Tony Robbins for your liking – write your three intentions down and stick them somewhere you will see them. On your mirror, on your fridge, on your desk. Feel them. Really feel them. Connect with them.

When you are intentional with your feelings and the way in which you exist, you can then be intentional with the bigger-picture stuff. The intention-setting and goal space, the manifesting, the vision boards. ALL OF THAT. There are enough YouTube videos and TikTok accounts to break down how to do this for you, so I won't waste your time right now because that's a different type of book. But I will encourage you to start with these micro-adjustments: they will set you on the path of living with great intention.

When it comes to this higher power I speak of – the universe, God or however you wish to refer to it – this element of spirituality may or may not resonate with you. If it doesn't, rather than picture in your head some old dude with a beard sitting up in heaven judging you, I want you to think of your higher power as an extension of yourself. Only you must always remember that ego and spirituality are not friends – you are not the universe and you most certainly are not God, but you're also not not.

RuPaul Charles once said that when they became spiritual it changed their life forever. In a conversation with Oprah as part of her *Super Soul Conversations* series, Ru said: 'The moment I became spiritual was the moment I realised that I am you and you are me and I am that tree over there and the tree is me, and

I am my neighbour and my neighbour is me. All of it is you. You are all of it. In hurting yourself you hurt them and in hurting them you hurt yourself.'

Let that marinate within you for a moment. To truly love yourself is to be gracious, and to lead with empathy and kindness. True self-love sits within. It sits in peace. It sits in confidence. It sits in divine respect of oneself.

I'm going to quote Dr Maya Angelou again: 'Find a place within yourself to remain clean. Keep it pristine and protected so that no one has the right to invade it.'

This is your spirit. This is devotion and self-love and worship. These are boundaries. This is your healing. Much like the use of a gym membership, my relationship with spirit ebbs and flows. I honestly couldn't tell you the last time I meditated for fifteen minutes like I used to in lockdown, but I set those foundations then, so that now I can vibrate at a higher frequency, my energy always listening, my spirit taking notice of the whispers before I lose them. My fierce devotional love for myself honours my boundaries in order to not let anyone invade my most sacred space.

You are a motherfucking goddess and your spirit is precious. Protect it fiercely. Let that space you've carved out be yours. Make room for love, but also make room for the love you so rightfully deserve, the same love you pour out freely into this world. Manifest it with great vigour.

I dedicated a whole wall in my bedroom to manifesting my partner Archie. I didn't know their name eight months ago, but the universe did, and when they showed up they were every single thing I had asked for on that wall. Open yourself up to great friendship and family and pleasure, and also to the possibility of pain, and all the things that simply come with the circle of life.

Be open to surrender always. Live on your knees rather than falling down to your knees only in prayer. When you exist in the space of surrender, magic happens. However, know that your internal compass, your heart space that is sacred – that's yours, darling. Worship it. Be devoted to it. Stay grateful for it. Love it. THIS IS SPIRITUALITY.

What a beautiful moment of worship this chapter has been. I feel like it's giving Sunday service. And just as all good sermons end, it's almost time for us to come together in song once more.

Over to you, darling

You might have a sense by now for how strongly I believe that gratitude and living with intention are essential conditions for living an authentic life. It can be tremendously difficult to stay grateful or to even see what we have around us to be grateful for, and when we miss cues for gratitude we default to feelings of absence and envy. When we train ourselves to default to feelings of gratitude, intention and abundance eventually follow.

Here's a simple exercise I'd like you to practise daily.

Step 1

Each morning after you've woken up, make your way outside if you have an area you can step into. If not, find yourself near a window. I find that just seeing the sky or looking outdoors helps to anchor me in these moments. Coffee in hand, think about three things you're grateful for. They could be as simple and obvious as waking up healthy, breathing and being alive. It could be the sun on your face, the chill in the air, the sound of running water as your partner showers, the smiles of your children or the pets in your home.

Step 2

Now that you've started to feel gratitude, I want you to set three simple intentions for your day. I often do this by picking three words to punctuate my day. For example, a go-to for me is 'Balance. Productive. Present.' If you'd like your intentions to be more specific, you could get more detailed. For example, 'Today I will write that email, make that call, start that exercise, finish that job, hit my daily target, make budget, take a walk, call my best friend, pick up that dry cleaning', etc.

If you want to keep it to the words, simply say out loud something like this to incorporate them within an intentional framework:

Universe, today I will strike the balance, I will be productive and I will remain present throughout each movement. I thank you in advance for the day ahead and the intentions you bless me with.

A daily practice that connects you to the universe and your spirit is always a good idea.

Step 3

This one's for night-time. As you get into bed and close your eyes, no matter how your day has played out, I can assure you there will be three simple things you can find gratitude in. Reflect on those three things. Some people write them down on paper, in a journal or even on the notes in your phone. By the end of the week you will have a whole list of things you were grateful for. Honestly, the perspective this will bring you on the abundance that already exists in your life is quite extraordinary.

The way in which these three simple, quick practices can shift your daily perspective is incredibly powerful. Lean into it, darlings.

🦌 Dance break 🦌

'Firework' – Katy Perry

This song, this sentiment, this video, makes me think of every one of us who starts our lives as a young person, filled with so much beautiful innocence and hope. A bright future is all too often darkened by the unfortunate environments the world will find us in. But as corny as this will sound, that light, that spirit: it's always been inside every one of us. It's time to let it out, darling. One step at a time.

The answer was always in you, Little Deni

It was my first webinar with Elise and this new 'Practice' community I was a part of. I was excited but also really fucking nervous. Truth be told, I was never great at meditating for long periods of time. I've always struggled switching off and disconnecting from the million and eleventy thoughts running through my overactive mind at any given time. Activities feel meditative to me, but actual meditation not so much.

Our meditation session began with Elise guiding us for a long walk through a beautiful green garden. I remember her instructing us to sit under a big great tree that she described. Opposite the tree was a beautiful lake for us to look towards. Guided meditations typically take five or so minutes to settle into, to get you to a place of deep surrender where you feel as though you are, in fact, walking through a garden. I was surprised at just how present I felt in that moment, with no external thoughts flooding their way in. It was amazing.

I couldn't tell you what this meditation focused on or which layer of spirit we were targeting that night, but what I can remember is exactly how that garden appeared and the way I looked in it, sitting by the tree.

The first thing I noted as I walked into the garden space was the long, free-flowing grass beneath and around my feet. It felt soft and lush. White flowing fabric cascaded its way around me, picking up on the sleeve length of the garment I was wearing. It sat just above my wrists, my fingers poking through. No acrylic nails. Just me, naked, bathed in white.

As I got closer to the tree, it reminded me of the same tree I'd sat under in Sydney, the one that united me with a plastic bag and ultimately opened me up to my first moment of surrender. Only that this tree was even bigger and grander in its presence. It felt familiar, like I had been here before.

When my view panned up from above, I noticed that I was wearing a white cotton gown, a beautiful cloth dress that felt both masculine and feminine all at once. It reminded me of the white cotton dress my mother and auntie made for me to wear to the Christmas concert. It felt like an elevated, more mature, grown-up, self-assured version of that dress. As I walked my way to the tree in Elise's meditation, I felt ethereal. I felt affirmed. I felt whole.

It was at that moment I knew for sure that my authentic self had always been deep inside of me, willing my spirit to let it out. I realised that, in fact, my authentic self was always there, only it had become buried over many years of social conditioning through a religious upbringing, gendered stereotypes and the opinions of others – but had been waiting for its release. And here, in a meditation with Elise via fucking Zoom, on a cool night in lockdown, my spirit showed me who I really was when no one was watching. Who I had always been. A genderfluid, ethereal goddess, with thick black hair and a white gown, cascading its way confidently and with ease around my calm spirit and bare feet.

I could cry just thinking about how empowering that moment of great sincere spirituality and devotion felt. Just my soul and me, and a beautiful white gown.

Affirmation

*Universe, I thank you so dearly for your presence in
    my life.*

I am grateful for your guidance.
I will listen to your whispers.
I welcome your support and trust in your spirit.

Thank you for walking inside and alongside me.
I love you.

10.

Power in liberation

There was no doubt in my mind that we would end here. How can any person live a truly authentic life without first liberating themselves from the many shackles, categories and systems the world has boxed us into? Honey, I am all for a little bondage and some light silk rope play, when consensual of course, but as for being tied to an ideology that doesn't serve me? No thank you, sir – there's nothing sexy about that.

When I look over the trajectory of my life thus far, I can think of many moments of true liberation. From that Christmas concert, my debut in a dress, to the time I was cast as a very outwardly Queer-presenting party planner in my school's Year 11 adaptation of *Cinderella*. I played the role of 'Pierre' from Paris, with a limp wrist and pastel-pink beret to boot. Singing Mariah Carey on my school stage was liberating, no matter how much bullying came after. Moving to Paris to study fashion liberated me to no end, as did my journeys to London and to Sydney. Getting my driver's licence felt liberating, as did landing my first job at the bakery. Marching in my first Sydney Mardi Gras was a liberating experience that I'm not sure can be matched. After having spent your whole life crucified by society for who you are, to then have thousands of people cheer for your identity is liberation personified.

When I became the last standing fashion editor in *Cosmopolitan Australia*'s history, knowing that I had been trusted with that role was peak career liberation. Though in many ways, rather ironically, being made redundant from the very same job felt liberating too. I've always felt that healthy forms of fear can liberate us, especially if we come to understand that those feelings are in fact nerves, which can lay the groundwork for excitement.

Coming out as gay at nineteen was liberating beyond measure, until twelve years later, when I found myself coming out once more as non-binary. A liberation that I never even knew existed.

I have been liberated many times over and I hope that the sense of liberation never stops informing who I am and how I move through this world. It is in liberation that I have found power and, alongside it, deep vulnerability.

When was the last time you felt truly liberated? Has fear held you back from its power? Have your environment and lived experience created roadblock after obstacle, liberty feeling like nothing but a hopeless dream? My hope is that this chapter brings you closer to your own feelings of liberation. I'll be standing by the sidelines cheering for you, darling.

But first, let me welcome you into my space. I really wish there was a way that I could see you in yours. That sounds creepier than I would have liked, but we're friends now. I've bared my soul to you and you have trusted me with yours. Maybe take a cute selfie or show me where you are reading this last chapter. Post it to your Instagram stories and tag me @stylebydeni so that you too can invite me in. I can't wait to see who is out there reading this book.

I am currently wearing a pair of grey marle Bonds trackies and a Beyoncé merch top from her *Black Is King* film. I have black Versace slippers on my feet and it's getting a little colder as I write this, as autumn well and truly makes its Victorian debut after a warmer than usual start to the year. I have a glass of water by my side for a change; Archie's influence is to thank for that.

By the time this book is finished, I will be living in Barwon Heads, with Archie and 'our' two cats, Taika and Khan. The universe has a funny way of placing you in the most unexpected spaces, right when you need them. You see, I had every intention of moving to Melbourne this year. Living my Carrie Bradshaw solo apartment fantasy, sweaters stored in the oven, boyfriend over for cute times and great sex. However, I found myself craving some balance away from the hustle and bustle of Melbourne and work trips to Sydney. I found that every time I drove over the West Gate Bridge and made my way to Geelong from the city, I exhaled sighs of relief. Archie felt the same. So we decided it was time we both honoured our mind, soul and vessels with a much-needed sea change. In fact as I write this I am currently sitting on the balcony of our new beach shack. The sun is warm on my cheeks and there is a massive palm tree in our backyard. My mind feels shiny. Life feels good.

I feel as though this will be my next season of true liberation. A space I can call my own, a family Archie and I are carving out together, an environment I can make mine, rent that I can finally afford to pay, without making SOS phone calls to my parents for a loan and without pulling up the Wallet Wizard website. Not anymore, my darling. I can proudly say that for the first time in my life I am financially independent and secure. A feeling so liberating it inspires me to work harder than I did yesterday and never find myself in the financial insecurity I once walked through.

Liberation comes in many different forms.

Did you know that only twenty-five years ago it was illegal to be gay in Australia? Tasmania was the last state to decriminalise homosexuality in 1997. Isn't that fucked? Only five years ago it was illegal for gay people to be married in this country. Imagine having to march through the streets of your home city – which for me at that time was Sydney, one of the gay capitals of the world – to protest for your right to marry. I will never forget the way that the same-sex marriage vote rippled its way through the public discourse of our entire country.

Here are memories from that time that stand out to me. One Thursday night after drinks with some mates at the pub, I hopped into an Uber to make my way home. My driver told me he would be voting no. He had brought up the subject to begin with. I told him he should be ashamed of himself and that he needed to pull the car over immediately. I got out and walked the rest of the way in tears.

On another occasion, my ex-boyfriend and I were playing tennis at some courts in Woollahra, a very bougie suburb in the east. Next to us was a family of four. Midway through our game, I looked up at the sky and saw a signwriting plane spelling out the word VOTE. I looked over at my boyfriend and said, 'Oh my god, it's going to say Vote Yes,' to which he said, 'I wouldn't be so sure, Deni.' We watched in horror as it began to spell the word NO.

The family on the court next to us were watching too. One of the kids asked their mum what the message meant; the mother looked over at us briefly and turned to her children. 'Just ignore that,' she told them. I immediately picked up my tennis racquet and told my boyfriend I wanted to leave. It felt like our very identities were being judged by our nation.

But against that backdrop of fear and anguish, Queer people and our allies by the thousands took to the streets in protest, marching for our right to equality. And the morning that the result was announced was another moment I won't soon forget. As I stood there in Prince Alfred Park surrounded by droves of Queer people, I remember Magda Szubanski, iconic comedian and LGBTQIA+ activist, standing on the stage with a microphone in her hands, a look of worry all over her face. As we waited for the result, I turned to my friend standing next to me and said, 'What if it's a no?' The result came a mere seconds later, seconds that felt like hours. It was a YES.

I dropped to my knees in a flood of tears. I phoned Mum and cried, 'I can get married one day. I'm allowed to get married too one day.' While on the call, an elderly lesbian wrapped her arms around me shouting, 'Your son's gonna get married one day, Mum!' 'Love Is in the Air' by John Paul Young played over a set of speakers at the park. As I hung up I saw a gay man in front of me propose to his partner in front of the crowd. Everywhere I looked there were people crying and embracing and kissing and celebrating the basic human right that is love. It was a moment of great liberation – from a fight that began long before we all came to stand there.

The gay liberation movement rose to prominence in the United States in the late 1960s, though there had been the seeds of earlier social protest movements across the US and Europe in the preceding decades. The movement urged lesbians, gays and trans folks to engage in radical direct action, and to counter societal shame with gay pride. The Stonewall riots in New York

City in 1969 sparked a global movement. Two important figures who featured in that uprising were trans women of colour. Their names were Marsha P. Johnson and Sylvia Rivera. In a moment of fear, anger and self-defence, Marsha threw that first brick at the police and chose liberation: not only to liberate herself but also the community she so proudly belonged to. When I reflect on the rights that I have today as both a trans/non-binary human and a gay one, it is because those who walked before me put their lives at risk to fight a battle much bigger than any one person alone.

Other mass protests, including the sustained power of the Black Lives Matter and feminist movements, reveal that we are stronger as a collective, and true power in liberation comes when people gather, arm in arm, to fight for the greater good. To fight so that one day their children and their children's children don't have to. So that one day all humans can feel truly liberated in their identity, so that they can live their lives without feeling as though they are carrying the weight of the world's judgement and scrutiny on their shoulders.

Liberation comes in many different forms. Collective liberation, my darlings, is merely one of them.

Acknowledging the power of liberty doesn't mean we shouldn't acknowledge how rooted in anguish it can be. For every group of humans gathered in protest, fighting for their community, members of that community elsewhere are on an individual level experiencing extreme disconnection and loneliness, or fates much worse. Liberation is in many ways a privilege. To this day, in some countries it is still illegal to be homosexual. In recent months we've seen the US Supreme Court's overturning of the *Roe v Wade* decision, which has stripped humans all over America of their safety, choice and personal autonomy.

There are so many layers to liberation as a state and as a process: for example, you can be liberated in one way at a macro level but feel trapped on a micro level. One may be out and proud about their sexual orientation or gender identity but continue to feel deeply insecure about their body, their race or social class. They might feel trapped. Claustrophobic. Stifled. Unable to be who they truly are. Personal liberation almost never comes all at once.

For almost all my adult life, the number one thing that has made me feel inferior, inadequate, less beautiful even, is the size and shape of my body. Just recently, I attended a fancy-schmancy event kicking off Melbourne's Grand Prix. I had loaned a dress from a designer friend of mine to wear, knowing full well that it was likely a size or two smaller than my frame. I figured I would just wear two pairs of spanx, but I felt uncomfortable in the dress from the moment I put it on. I felt uncomfortable in the car ride there. I felt uncomfortable on the media wall, sucking my 'belly' in for the entirety of the red carpet, unable to concentrate fully on which photographer to look at and more distracted by whether I would look 'fat' in these photos. I carried a generously sized clutch for the remainder of the night in front of my midsection.

I was the only masc-presenting human at this event in a dress, heels and a full face of make-up, but that didn't bother me at all. In fact, it didn't even cross my mind. While I stood there, in a sea of sample-size humans, standing liberated in pride of my gender identity and Queerness, I simultaneously felt further away from body liberation than I have in a long time.

You wanna know what's helped me in liberating myself from my body? Like-minded humans who proudly and vocally share their own body journeys online. To feel truly liberated doesn't come without moments of discomfort, but if I aim to feel even 40 percent liberated in my own skin on any given day, I know that the following day, I can throw in another 10 percent, and then another twenty the day after, and then before I even realise it there are moments where I stand so firm in liberation that I love and honour my body and vessel for what it is and the strength that exudes from the outside in.

Liberation is not linear, and then sometimes, it comes all at once and crashes over you like a wave in the ocean. I had one such moment the first time I put on heels as an adult.

It was a Friday night. My boyfriend at the time invited me to his friend's house for drinks. Upon arrival, I was greeted at the door by my boyfriend in a long red silk robe that swept behind him. On his feet was a pair of heels I had never seen him in, so I was taken aback for a moment. In a very good way. As I turned the corner and made my way into the large open living and dining room I observed as a gaggle of gays filled the space, each with some form of costume draped around them. Some in slightly more subtle choices, while others opted for bold headpieces and wigs. Each of them, however, stood firmly in pride. Comfortable in their own skin.

Our host poured me a cocktail and it didn't take long for him and my boyfriend to usher me to the costume box. Something I now know almost every gay man to have, in some capacity. If you search through the wardrobes of gay men the world over, I can practically guarantee you there will be a costume box, big or small. Some of my friends have entire rooms dedicated to costumes and, honestly, I love that for them.

We made our way into a perfectly sized walk-in robe and sat down on the floor, cross-legged like high school girls, around this costume box. Our host asked with great enthusiasm the question I'd been dreading: 'Deni, what will you choose?' When I was in kindergarten, my mother was told by my teacher that it was 'a problem' I always chose the girl's side of the costume rail. Suffice to say that childhood trauma had lodged in my subconscious for quite some time.

I found myself rummaging through the box with trepidation, looking for the most masculine thing I could find. My boyfriend could sense my nerves. Taking my hand gently, he passed over a black bodysuit; it had a sort of wet look to it and a zipper that ran all the way up the torso. Very Beyoncé 'Single Ladies' energy. He fished further into the box and pulled out, in all their glory, a pair of black patent PVC stiletto sandals. Think stripper shoes meets drag queen heel essential. They were high enough to intimidate me, but not as high as you might see at your local drag or strip show.

'Put them on, babe. They'll look amazing on you.' I froze for a moment. My boyfriend was asking me to put on a pair of heels, to wear in front of a house full of his friends who I was only just meeting for the first time. Not only was he asking me, he was *encouraging* me to do so. The feeling was foreign but one I welcomed with quiet gusto. As I strapped myself into the heels and poured myself into the black fitted jumpsuit, I looked at the mirror and almost didn't recognise the reflection.

Except that I did. This Deni had always been inside of me, they just never felt as though they were allowed to come out. I made my way into the dining room to roars of applause from the group and surprised even myself at just how well I could walk in the stilettos. My whole face went red with glee. All it took was a tequila shot and a room full of encouragement and, before I knew it, I was serenading them all with a dance performance to 'Single Ladies' by Beyoncé. Because you can take the performer off the stage, but you can't take the stage out of this performer. In that moment, in a pair of nine-centimetre PVC stilettos and a bodysuit, I felt more liberated than I'd ever been in my life. For all the difficulties in that relationship, I will forever be grateful to him for playing an integral role in the liberation of my gender identity. In that moment, it was a feeling like no other.

So I didn't.

My penchant for fabulous heels didn't continue all at once, but I did begin to drip-feed them into my wardrobe, exclusively at gay clubs and dress-up parties. Another thing you should know about Queer humans is that they love a fucking dress-up party. Following my dining room debut, Halloween was fast approaching and in planning my look for another gay house party, one of oh so many, I landed on a pair of clear PVC ankle boots. Kanye West had just released a pair for his increasingly popular brand Yeezy and I'd managed to find a dupe online for a fraction of the cost from a high street retailer. I wore them with black tights and danced the night away in them.

My love and, frankly, addiction to heels continued and every single costume party thereafter would include a new heel purchase. The more I wore them, the more liberated I felt. I even marched in Mardi Gras in heels that year. They were bright red ankle boots covered from heel to toe in glitter, my very own version of a 'Dorothy' shoe. I made my way somewhere over the rainbow, and I did so for two kilometres up Oxford Street, thank you very much.

However, my heeled outings were acceptable in night-time party environments only. I never dared to pop down to brunch in a pair of stilettos, because that wouldn't be seen as appropriate. What would people say? What would they think of me? Would I be heckled? There's a pattern here of feeling liberated yet stifled simultaneously, a difficult dichotomy to navigate. When in one moment a space can make you feel liberated enough to express your true self yet can also stifle you, clip your wings.

It's for this very reason that so many people feel safe exclusively in environments that foster such feelings, ranging from a Queer-filled dining room in Paddington to a gay club on Oxford Street; your best friend's couch or perhaps your therapist's office. It is why so many people feel as though they have to behave one type of way at work and can only truly be themselves outside of office hours.

In my career I have watched as women especially, in female-dominated workspaces, can sit in editor's chairs and feel completely empowered, yet the mere presence of their husbands sees them revert to submissive behaviours they would never display among the teams they lead. I've seen this play out on more than one occasion, often wishing that equal liberation could be experienced at all times in all spaces. Maybe that's terribly hopeful and idealistic of me. But wouldn't it be nice if we could feel power in our liberation no matter where we are?

This is a feeling I set out to continue beyond the walls of my family's home after lockdown. I made a promise to myself: if I could feel comfortable throwing on a pair of heels at 11 am to make a TikTok video at home, I would liberate myself with the freedom to wear heels to brunch.

So I did.

On the first morning of freedom, after what felt like the longest of Victorian lockdowns, I met my friends at my family's cafe for a late breakfast and strutted in wearing a pair of boyfriend jeans, a sweater and a new pair of heels I acquired during lockdown. It was a first for me and fuck, it felt thrilling. Those heels were going to walk their way into cafes and supermarkets and lean into the liberation I had honoured myself with.

Liberation doesn't arrive via our sartorial choices alone. It also arrives through the much deeper ways in which we choose to live our lives.

How many people have you observed staying in relationships that they know are no longer serving them? In jobs they hate. Living with housemates they don't like. Keeping friendships that don't fulfil them. Surrounded by family members who don't value or affirm them. Sticking to diets that spark self-loathing. Living in all but a constant state of self-loathing. You may yourself be such a person. I have been too. We all have been.

Here is where I would like you to begin. I want you to stop for a moment and ask yourself:

Do I feel liberated in my life and identity?
When was the last time I felt truly liberated?

If the answer to the first question is no and the second is so long ago that you can't remember, or possibly even never – I want you to ask yourself, WHY?

What is it that's holding you back from truly liberating yourself with radical self-love and acceptance? Because you know by now that this is the key: liberation comes from within, when we are truly at peace with ourselves. Some will travel halfway across the world to find this state of mind. Others will make the pilgrimage to bigger cities where they feel as though they can be themselves. Some find subcultures and communities they can become a part of either digitally or IRL in order to feel accepted and find a sense of belonging. Others will look for liberation in the partners they choose to share their lives with, the families they choose to create for themselves and the careers they work hard to throw themselves into at full force. God knows I've done all the things listed above, and while these methods can be truly soul-serving exercises, it is inside yourself alone that you can truly find this liberty.

So I want you to get curious, darling. I want you to dig deep, to sit in the shadows and enquire within to connect the dots. Let's continue with another round of questions. These may take some homework and time for you to answer honestly.

Over to you, darling

1. How has your childhood influenced who you are today and the ways in which you feel right now?
2. How have your family and culture formed your identity and the way you feel about yourself, either positively or negatively?
3. What are the roles that conformity and nonconformity have played in either liberating or stifling your authentic self?

4. How have sex, sexuality and shame factored into the overall equation of your identity and relationship with it?

5. What about love, relationships and all matters of the heart? What role have they played in shaping your life and who you are today?

6. How have your job, career and/or lack thereof moulded the person you are and the way you feel about your life?

7. How about body image and self-worth? Where do you sit on the scale of acceptance when it comes to your physical vessel and which of these factors have influenced the way you feel about yourself?

8. What role has the environment in which you exist in informed your identity? Be it your home or the city, state or country you live in. Is the environment in which you spend most of your time fostering a fulfilling relationship with yourself and your identity?

9. How is your spirit? Do you feel connected to it? Are you letting your intuition guide you, or has life become one tick box after another of things you feel as though you're forced to tick? Are your identity, intuition and spirit aligned and are they honouring each other?

10. Do you feel fucking liberated?

It is my hope that the little pop quiz above has made it very clear for you to see the reasons why you might not be feeling liberated so that you can start the long and rewarding process to get there.

Bonus points for those of you who realised that I have just outlined every chapter of this book. I knew when I mapped out the chapters that, in order to reach this final destination of liberation, every other pillar of life had to first be rigorously assessed, broken down and brought together. But with that said, the truth of the matter is that liberation is not a read-this-book-and-you're-fixed kinda destination. It is in many cases a lifelong process of inquiry, and great analysis, and sitting in the shadows, and looking inwards, and really holding yourself accountable to the life that you are living.

People often look at me and say words like *brave, strong, authentic, inspiring, bold, bright, confident.* While all of those things might be true, I can promise you that they're not true all at once. They take work, often over days, months, sometimes years, of unpacking and working through trauma. Fighting off one intrusive thought and insecurity after the last.

My aim with this book was to offer you a lifelong guidebook. I want you to return to it, to go back to sections that most resonate with the season of life in which you find yourself. In one moment you might find yourself absolutely slaying the career and relationship pillars of your identity while also navigating self-worth and shame simultaneously. There is a quote that instantly comes to mind by one of my all-time favourite Real Housewives, Chyka Keebaugh, from the Melbourne franchise. I'm sure the quote is not her own but in one particular season, her tagline goes as follows:

'You can have it all, just not all at once.'

... and honestly, spit the truth, sis. Never has a cliché been more appropriate.

There is no single human who at any given time can feel all the victorious feelings simultaneously. Even Beyoncé has her off days, honey. So when I tell you that life's true joy comes in the knowing that we are all works in progress, I mean it.

It should also be said that liberation can arrive in the most microscopic of changes, and those are just as worthy of celebrating as macro changes are. In fact, they are even more worthy of our celebration because they can be harder to execute. Maybe, just maybe, tomorrow you'll finally reply to your condescending colleague's email with confidence and conviction. No 'kind regards' necessary. Fuck, you might walk straight into your boss's office and finally ask for the pay rise you deserve. You might turn to your partner in bed tonight and communicate to them that something they said at dinner really upset you. You might turn to them and express, finally, that you are feeling undervalued or unfulfilled in your relationship. Heck, you might even break up with them.

You might finally reactivate that Hinge profile, because honestly what is holding you back, Queen? You might set a boundary with your sister and tell her she's no longer welcome to eat those fucking Doritos in your brand-new car on the way home from work. You might finally set a boundary with your best friend – you know, the kind of boundary you've let slide because of behaviour you've for years just accepted. You might google that pottery class you've always dreamed of taking but felt as though you weren't good enough to. Maybe you'll change your uni degree or drop out of uni altogether, because it's really just not for you and you can't spend another five years at school for a career your parents want you to complete.

Maybe you'll push yourself out of your comfort zone and wear that dress you've been too scared to try. You might build up the courage to put on lipstick even though you're anxious it will clash with your thick beard. Perhaps you'll book that therapist's appointment or download the Headspace app. Maybe you'll finally give meditation a try, even for five minutes. You might finally sit down with your mother and start to slowly unpack childhood trauma she inflicted. That's no small feat, but it could start with an action as mundane as pouring a cup of fresh Moccona.

 Over to you, darling

Five easy ways to make meditation a daily practice:

The concept of meditation used to overwhelm me. Visions of sitting down in silence for thirty minutes at a time, chanting OHM while incense burns, wasn't really my vibe. What I've learnt with the help of Elise is that meditation can look, feel and sound different to many people. The key to the practice is to find yourself present in the moment.

Tip 1

It doesn't need to take more than five minutes. Seriously. Three to five minutes is better than none at all. The goal of meditation is not how long you do it for, but rather the quality of your practice. Five minutes can go a long way.

Tip 2

Find a way that meditation can be integrated into your routine that doesn't feel like a chore. You know how you put off going to the gym in winter because it's much warmer in your bed and you have to get up and drive ten minutes down the road? You don't want to make meditating feel like that. Could your meditation practice occur while making your morning coffee or even while in the shower? It's no coincidence that I often have the best ideas in the shower because my mind is at peace: water is gushing down on me, and my headspace is free. Make it work for you, not against you.

Tip 3

Listen and feel. You can do this with the help of free guided meditations online, but you can just as easily do it without. I used to sit outside, with my morning coffee, the family dog by my side, and just be still. I'd shut my eyes.

The first thing I'd do was listen to what was around me, noticing the sounds of the wind, any neighbours in the distance, a bus pulling up on my street. *Listen*. Then I want you to feel. Can you feel the sun on your face, the hair of your dog at your fingertips, the chill of the air on your pinky toe peeking from your slippers? *Feel*. See what drops in: you might hear thoughts, you might see visuals. Ideas may start to drop in. Memories. Tastes. Songs. You'd be surprised what comes up in meditation. Let it all drop in.

Tip 4

Now, depending on where you are, take a moment after your meditation to reflect on what came up and what it might mean to you. Write it down if that helps.

Tip 5

Rinse and repeat. You don't need to do this every day, but even if you allocate three times a week to meditating, your mind will be better for it. If you want to take it one step further, you may want to start a meditation journal. Journalling what those feelings and thoughts are straight after can be a really helpful way of reflecting on your meditation and seeing how your practice and mindset evolve over time. Do what feels right for you.

Meditation is important because it allows time for you to sit and be with yourself, to listen to the whispers and check in with your authentic core to assess how you're feeling. The reason we so often veer off course is because we spend nowhere near enough time prioritising self-reflection.

You are the MVP of your team, so make time for you. Please. K, love you.

If I can even remotely inspire you to just do one small thing that will liberate you in this very moment, then that is my job done. Do the small thing! Then, let's keep doing the next small thing and then the next one and then make the one after that a medium-size thing and then the next time add a third, and then before you know it you will take a moment to reflect on the many micro-adjustments you have taken charge of so as to fully form your liberation towards LIVING AUTHENTICALLY.

It is my hope that all those small things lead to life-changing moments of clarity.

Dance break

It feels only fitting that we wrap the last chapter of the book in a big bow of freedom with an absolute anthem. One of the first times I truly understood the power of the lyrics to the song we're about to play was New Year's Eve in 2018 when I was at Tropical Fruits, an incredible festival founded by Queer trailblazers in the beautiful town of Lismore in New South Wales.

Lismore has been home to Tropical Fruits since it started in 1988, the same year I was born. Cut to some twenty-six years later, as the clock struck midnight, me and a few thousand Queers made our way back from the fairground, where we had watched fireworks burst out all over the sky, to the dancehall to party our way into the first morning of a new year. In the hall I could hear the beginning of a very familiar beat, and as if on cue when we entered, the DJ played the famous introductory keys to a song we all intimately knew.

I looked around that hall as we danced, at the Queer humans around me, basking in their liberation. I held back tears, thinking, *This is what George meant*. Little did I know there were many more experiences of true liberation waiting on the road ahead of me.

Ready. Set. Press Play.
'Freedom! '90' – George Michael

Affirmation

I am grateful for the journey I have been blessed with.
Every up and every down. Every challenge and every joy.

I make peace with the crossroads moments that have led me here.
I make peace with each pillar of my identity, knowing that I am a work in progress.

I rejoice in the work.

I celebrate the liberation I give myself.
I am a divine creation and am worthy of celebration.

I relish in my authentic self.
With adoration and respect.

I continue to prioritise growth, healing and evolution.
Infinitely so.

I love you, boo.
We've got this, now and forevermore.

Epilogue

You did it, darling. We did it. We've arrived at the end of our journey together. How are you feeling: Inspired? Exhausted? Overwhelmed? Excited but also unsure what to do next? All of the above?

Me too, hun.

Writing this book has been one of my most treasured life experiences, and though it's involved many head-scratching, tired-eye-twitching hours of my life, I will forever cherish this memory. In setting out to write this book, my intention was to inform and inspire. To educate and be educated. Within these pages I have learned so much about myself and the people around me. I hope you have too.

I told you in the introduction that the premise of this book was to arm you with the tools to REWRITE THE RULES AND LIVE AUTHENTICALLY. You know what? I have a spoiler to share with you:

The truth about finding our authentic selves is that it's a journey that no one book, or exercise, meditation or vision board, can map out in any one-size-fits-all way. The journey towards finding our authentic selves is much like the ongoing journey of me (re)discovering my gender identity. There isn't a clear destination or prescriptive process, nor is the journey defined by binary limits of good/bad, authentic/inauthentic.

Bear with me as I talk for a moment in theatre metaphors. You know by now that I'm a stage kid at heart, and I bloody love a metaphor, so here we go.

Life is not a dress rehearsal, but it's also not any one show. It's a series of performances we endlessly repeat and persevere through, no matter the ups and downs. It's the show you take after the breakout role. It's the role in the niche off-Broadway show you've just been cast in, the one that only a select few may attend. It's the performance in the production you least expected you'd take but honestly really needed the money that season. It's the meeting you had with your agent last week and the casting you attended, only to be rejected.

The shows, the roles, the venues, that stage, the auditions, those performances, they never really stop. Until, of course, our time is up, and then honestly who knows what the next act looks like. (I hope it features a very camp devil and 'Montero' by Lil Nas X, to be honest – but you get what I'm saying.)

The discovery of our authentic self exists in every single space in between. It exists not only in the moment the curtain is drawn, the light hits your face and you say your first line, but also in the moments leading up to that one.

It exists in the steps you take when you leave the theatre and you thank the stage manager, it exists in the moment you smile at the venue cleaner walking towards you with their cleaning trolley. The moment you thank the doorman and address the driver waiting for you in the Uber home. The moment you walk up the stairs into your building.

My hope is that having read this book, you may feel even a little more equipped to tackle all those moments in between. The uncomfortable fittings with a stylist who wants to push you into a costume that just doesn't fit right. The uncomfortable moments when your co-star or ensemble cast are just not bringing equal heart to the show's performance. The uncomfortable conversation you have with your agent when they tell you it's all about tall skinny redheads right now and you're just not hot this season, and every moment of discomfort that settles its way into the story of your life thereafter.

It is my hope that within the pages of this book and its stories, its exercises and advice, its laughs and tears alike, its wisdom from Elise and its dance breaks, that you find the tools to navigate through the story of your own life on your own fucking terms. For it is in all the mundane moments of practice that a star is truly born, and darling, we want you to shine brighter than the lights at the MCG.

Go be that star. Live with great intention. Refer back to your intention. Sit in the shadows, work towards your healing, honour your inner child and refer back to them with a remembrance that they have always known who you are. Commit to your daily practice knowing that you will fall on and off the bandwagon of internal care because, as my boyfriend would say, you're not a fucking robot, you're a human with feelings. You will fall off. We all do. So when you do, refer back to this ol' book. Perhaps to a quote that stood out. To the vision boards I want you to keep updating as your life continues to evolve. Go back to even the smallest exercise that might help you get back on again. Remembering always that falling off is okay.

Accept the unaccepted and celebrate every goddamn flaw, because all of it is you and all of it is love, and honey, self-love and radical self-acceptance and living authentically are the motherfucking MVPs here. You know this now, so go forth and conquer.

In the spirit of empathy, love and kindness, pay this knowledge forward. I am but a sum of the lessons I have learned from so many around me. If this book was helpful, if you had AHA! moments, epiphanies and revelations that led to liberation, spread that love far and wide. Pass it on to those you love. Authenticity shared is authenticity doubled, and frankly I couldn't think of anything more beautiful.

May we start a revolution of living authentically. Now isn't that a global show you'd love to star in? Oscar contender, if you ask me!

I love this for us and darling, truly, I LOVE THIS FOR YOU! Thank you. I love you.

x Deni

ACKNOWLEDGEMENTS

It is with the utmost gratitude and unconditional love that I must first thank and acknowledge my parents, Maca and Zlatko. It all begins with you two; it always will. Thank you for loving me unconditionally, and for encouraging my passions and celebrating them even when the world made fun of us. Thank you for buying me books and nurturing my love of reading and writing from as early as four. For buying me that sewing machine when I was in primary school, and letting me go study in Paris even though I knew you'd cry rivers, Mama. It is because of your hard work and every selfless act of love that you have blessed me with that I have had this extraordinary life. Thank you, Mama and Tata, for giving me your blessing to share so much of our own story in this book. I hope you know you're redefining what parenthood can look like for so many. I love you, all the way to the nebo (heavens) and infinitely more.

To my business partner, manager, mentor and chosen family, Pru Corrigan. Toots! What a fucking ride it's been. You took a

LOVE THIS FOR YOU

chance on this sassy non-binary kid dancing their way through lockdown and you opened your heart to the dream. You have changed my life in more ways than I could have ever fathomed and I am so grateful to have you in it. To the next mountain peak and every one thereafter, I'm so grateful that we're in this together. I love you. And to Anna Hays and the extended One Daydream team, you really are the dream team. Thank you infinitely for your love and support.

To Archie, my beloved. It's wild to think that when I got this book deal I didn't even know what your voice sounded like. Who knew you would be the first person I ever read my first chapter to. Thank you, dušo, for every ounce of support and love you have showered me with during this process. Thank you for coming into my life and showing me what love truly means. I love you. The most. And a special shout-out must go out to your family, the Boulter family, for all of your support and love throughout this process.

Speaking of family, to my brother Michael for putting your arm around me when I was a scared teenager coming out in our kitchen and for never letting go, thank you for the constant stream of love and support. To my sister-in-law Marija and my niece Sofia, the light of my life, I love you.

To my editor, Tom Langshaw. Fuck, darling, we did it! We've well and truly earned that dance at Palms. From that very first Zoom call in lockdown, I just knew you'd be the only human to edit my words and sit next to me on this car ride of writing a fucking book. Thank you for the level of genuine care and empathy, of support and love for every single word. From your attention to detail, to the safe space in which you provided me to pour my heart out, to the way in which you collaborate – you are one of a kind, my friend. Thank you. When do we start the next one? *No but really can you just be my editor forever? K thanks.*

To Ali Green and the extended Pantera Press team: I mean, talk about a dream publisher. Thank you for welcoming me into the Pantera family with such warmth and love. I bloody adore and respect each of you tremendously, and just feel so damn lucky to have got to do this with you.

To my dear friend, spiritual oracle guide and changer of lives, Elise. I could write essays on just how much you mean to me and how much you've enriched my life. Thank you for seeing my light on the couch that very first day, when I was questioning whether or not I had any light left within me. The universe put us in each other's path, and I am so grateful it did. Thank you for gifting this book with your words and wisdom and spirit. I love you, friend. A whole lot.

To George Saad for designing the cover of dreams, to Jes Layton for bringing my crossroads-fashion moments to life with your illustrations, to Cristina Briones for your copyedit and to Camha Pham for your proofread, to my friends Monika Berry for shooting the back cover image and Tess Holmes for the beat. To my darling Jane Negline, I love you – thank you for being the book publicist KWEEN. I am so honoured to have my words accompany such remarkable creatives.

To the exquisite Dannii Minogue, Narelda Jacobs, Mia Freedman, Maria Thattil, Michelle Andrews and Yumiko Kadota, thank you for taking the time to read this book before anyone else. Each of you know how much you inspire and mean to me (mostly because I'll never stop reminding you), and your support, love and feedback have been a gift I will forever treasure.

To all of my family and friends who have supported me throughout this chapter of my life, but especially to my dead-body friends. Amanda, Lisa, Riley, Tay, Jemma, Jess, Carly and Emily – thank you for every single 'How are you going with the writing, boo?' text. All the check-ins and support. The late-night virtual fist pumps and cheers of applause. For putting up with the many unread text messages, rescheduled catch-ups and general writing angst. You are my dead-body friends for a reason and I am so fucking grateful. Now we celebrate.

Finally, how could I ever find the adequate words to articulate just how much my community means to me. For every single darling who has followed along the journey, the humans who on a daily basis come to @stylebydeni with an open heart and mind, with empathy, love and kindness, with curiosity and candour – THANK YOU. It is because of you that I have been given this privilege and I am insurmountably grateful. You inspired this book and so this book is my gift to you. I hope you've enjoyed it as much as I have writing it. I love you, darlings.

'Self-made, self-motivated and infectiously self-assured, Flex plays both forthright coach and open-hearted student of life in this practical, empowered guide to achieving your own version of success.'

--- ZOË FOSTER BLAKE ---

'A joyful, confident, razor-sharp and exquisitely modern plan to creating success in a way that is meaningful to you.'

ZOË FOSTER BLAKE

THE SUCCESS EXPERIMENT

FLEXMAMI's formula for knowing what you really want and how to get it

LILLIAN AHENKAN

BUSINESS OWNER, PODCASTER, INFLUENCER, TV PRESENTER

PANTERA PRESS

SPARKING IMAGINATION, CONVERSATION & CHANGE